ALL
IN

Lucille Shackleton is an Australian sexologist and relationship therapist. At her private practice in Sydney, Lucille helps her clients create healthy relationships by supporting them to improve their relationship, both with themselves and their partner/s. Her approach is rooted in empathy, a deep understanding of self, and a firm belief in the power of willingness. Lucille has completed a Bachelor of Behavioural Science and postgraduate degrees in Psychosexual Therapy, Public Health and Counselling. Her writing is sought after and her Instagram @lucille.shackleton is often quoted in publications such as the *Sydney Morning Herald*, *Stylist*, *Huffington Post* and various international media outlets. Her insights and advice have become trusted resources for those navigating the complexities of love, intimacy and self-discovery. To learn more about Lucille visit lucilleshackleton.com.

ALL

Know yourself, transform your romantic
relationships and unlock great sex

IN

Lucille Shackleton

Sexologist and Relationship Therapist

PENGUIN BOOKS

UK | USA | Canada | Ireland | Australia
India | New Zealand | South Africa | China

Penguin Books is part of the Penguin Random House group of companies
whose addresses can be found at global.penguinrandomhouse.com.

Penguin
Random House
Australia

First published by Penguin Books in 2025

Cover design by Christabella Designs © Penguin Random House Australia Pty Ltd
Typeset in ITC Berkeley Oldstyle by Midland Typesetters, Australia

Printed and bound in Australia by Griffin Press, an accredited
ISO AS/NZS 14001 Environmental Management Systems printer

 A catalogue record for this
book is available from the
NATIONAL LIBRARY OF AUSTRALIA National Library of Australia

ISBN 978 1 76134 718 4

penguin.com.au

 MIX
Paper | Supporting
responsible forestry
FSC® C018684

We at Penguin Random House Australia acknowledge that Aboriginal and Torres Strait
Islander peoples are the Traditional Custodians and the first storytellers of the lands
on which we live and work. We honour Aboriginal and Torres Strait Islander peoples'
continuous connection to Country, waters, skies and communities. We celebrate
Aboriginal and Torres Strait Islander stories, traditions and living cultures;
and we pay our respects to Elders past and present.

To those who have loved, lost, healed and been brave enough to open up to love again. This book is for you. May you *be* and *create* the love you seek.

As the author of this book, I would like to acknowledge and pay my deepest respect to Aboriginal and Torres Strait Islander people across Australia. I express my sincerest gratitude to the traditional custodians of the lands, waters and skies where I live and work, and where this book was written. In particular, I recognise the Gadigal people of the Eora nation and the Palawa people of Lutruwita as well as the traditional owners of the land that you, the reader, are on. I honour the storytellers, the artists and all of the First Nations people who have cared for this land for generations. This always was and always will be, Aboriginal land.

Contents

Part Three All About Sex and Intimacy

Introduction

Great relationships are not found, they are co-created by the people in them. They are built moment by moment, choice by choice in the ways we show up and engage with one another, how we speak to one another, how we treat one another and even how we think about one another. Building safe, connected, loving and *conscious* relationships is an active process which requires us to learn how to honour ourselves while also honouring others. It requires us to know ourselves and our needs and to be mindful of the ways our past hurts influence how we engage in our romantic connections.

The trouble is, most of us were never taught how to do any of this. We weren't taught how to create safe love, how to use conflict as an opportunity for growth and knowing one another more deeply, or how to navigate our different needs.

That's why I'm here. My goal is to give you the knowledge, skills and tools to create safe and loving connections which will support your growth and healing both individually and together. I invite you to embark on a journey of self-discovery. Whether you're in a relationship or unattached, this book will help you better understand yourself and teach you how to navigate the complexities of romantic love.

All In is an opportunity to elevate your emotional connections and help you work through the patterns that may be keeping you stuck. It's an invitation to know yourself more deeply, to learn why you relate to others the way you do and to explore your sexual self.

You'll learn all the things I wish someone had taught me before I became a relationship therapist and sexologist, such as how to build safe, loving and healthy relationships with yourself and others. I'll provide you with moments to reflect; actionable advice to implement; as well as activities you can utilise straightaway. You'll find out how to fully invest in yourself, your relationships and, most importantly, how to go 'all in'.

But what exactly does that mean? Well, going 'all in' simply means being *willing* to fully invest in both yourself *and* your relationship. They go hand in hand. I emphasise 'willing' because in my work, both professionally and personally, I've found that *willingness* is what sets apart those who make change and improve their relationships and those who do not. Ultimately, it's a choice. A choice to show up, do the work and co-create conscious connections rather than just going through the motions and hoping things will change.

In order to go all in, we need to be willing to look at ourselves, how we engage in our relationships and how our baggage and 'stuff' contributes to the challenges we experience. That's what this book is about; bringing your attention back to your relationship with yourself, and learning what it takes to create and sustain a thriving relationship with others.

You'll hear the word 'willing' more times than I can count in this book! This is because no-one shows up to a relationship fully healed. No-one shows up without baggage and 'stuff' they need to work on. No-one can meet *all* of your needs . . . but the question is, are they *willing* to show up and grow the connection with you? Are they *willing* to create a space for a shared experience? Are they *willing* to do what it takes to create safe love?

In one way or another, we are all in 'relationship recovery'. We all have psychological wounds from our childhood we are trying to heal through our adult relationships. We all look to our partner/s to care for us in the ways we feel we were neglected as kids. If they struggle to do so we feel let down, abandoned, betrayed and often find ourselves reacting as if we were children again.

We are all imperfect. Relationships require us to do the work . . . together. No-one is immune because we all have to process and grieve the ways we have been hurt, moulded and conditioned throughout our lives. Most of us have little conscious awareness of how these experiences affect us, of how they determine our needs and behaviours. We simply go along, oblivious to how big a part our conditioning, childhood and past relational hurts actually play in our relationship issues.

I can't tell you how many people come to therapy hoping their therapist will just agree with them and say their partner is wrong and should change. We are blinded by our subjective reality and often believe it's them, not us. In this book, I'm not going to tell you how to change your partner/s. What I will do is help you learn about yourself, understand why you show up and engage in relationships the way you do, and give you the opportunity to create the partnership you *want* to experience. I will teach you about safe love, how to create a conscious relationship and how to deepen intimacy. If that sounds like what you're looking for, then you've come to the right place.

Throughout the book, I'll use real examples to describe a topic and drive a point home. All of the examples have been created by me and are composites representing themes I see in my therapy practice, the conversations I have about relationships, and the many DMs I receive on social media. None of these examples reflects any one person's experience but rather demonstrates the issues that I see coming up again and again. I will also share my own personal stories and experiences because I think it's only fair that if we're going on this journey together you learn a little bit about your guide! I am a sexologist and relationship therapist, but I am also someone who has had long-term committed relationships and short dating experiences. I have had relationships with people of different genders. I have had great, healthy relationships and, unfortunately, I have also had an abusive relationship.

I share all of this because I believe my personal experiences – along with my training and clinical practice – put me in a unique position. I think it helps me understand and relate to the challenges you face and hopefully will allow me to give you what you both want and need from this book.

In saying that, I must also acknowledge my privilege. I am a white, cisgender woman who, while not straight, benefits from straight privilege as I am straight passing. I grew up in Sydney where I had the privilege of being able to access higher education. And I am very aware of how all of these factors have benefited me throughout my life.

I have tried to make this book as inclusive as possible, but the reality is, the elements that influence how we show up in relationships (culture, trauma, family of origin, gender, race, religion, and so forth) mean it cannot be *entirely* inclusive, not least because most relationship research is based on heterosexual, neurotypical and monogamous couples. With that in mind, I have done my best to provide information and tools which apply to a wide variety of circumstances. I hope that regardless of whether you're in a monogamous relationship, an open relationship, a polycule relationship, or are single, separated, or just looking to deepen your connection with yourself, you will take something valuable from this book.

The one thing I need from you is an open mind. *All In* is not for those who are unwilling to look at themselves and go deep. It's for the brave, for the adventurous, for those who are ready to explore why they are the way they are, and why they relate the way they do. I am passionate about this reflective process which is why the book begins with an examination of your beliefs about relationships.

Part one is all about you. You'll learn how your ideas and expectations about relationships were formed. You'll discover your 'attachment style' and the essential ingredients for safe love before exploring how your emotions affect your relationships. We'll then move on to specific tools and strategies that will help you navigate common relationship challenges.

In part two, the focus is on how you come together and co-create a great relationship. You'll learn how to build a conscious relationship, how to navigate issues and manage conflict productively. Part two gives you the tools and strategies to begin the work on fixing and rebuilding an already established connection – or constructing the foundations from the ground up.

Finally, in part three we'll get to sex! The last section of the book will involve a bit of re-education. We'll start with an exploration of your sexual history and how it affects the way you think about sex, then work on liberating you from the expectations of how things *should* be so you can start focusing on pleasure.

All In is not about me coming to you as an expert. It's about me, a fellow human who wants to share what I have learned from both my professional and personal experience in the hope it will benefit you. I have tried to write from a place of inclusivity and openness. It is not my role nor my desire to prescribe any one kind of relationship structure. Instead, I hope that the information and tools in this book will help you create secure, connected foundations in whatever relationship structure works for you.

My goal is that *All In* will help you to grow, learn and improve your connection with yourself and elevate your relationships with others. I have called it *All In* because you can't do this work with one foot out the door. You have to be willing to fully invest in the process.

So, if you're ready . . . let's dive all in!

PART ONE

ALL ABOUT YOU

1
Beliefs

What were you taught about relationships?

Have you ever wondered why you are the way you are? Or why you relate the way you do? The answer is simple: it's down to your beliefs. And those beliefs are 'socially conditioned'. To put it simply, the messages we receive from society and culture shape – or rather, condition – our thoughts, feelings, values, behaviours and attitudes.[1]

This all happens through the positive and negative reinforcements we receive and it starts from the moment we are born. As children, we receive positive reinforcement when we behave in socially acceptable ways and negative reinforcement when we behave in socially unacceptable ways. This in turn moulds how we behave in the future. Social conditioning occurs within our families, communities, schools, workplaces, social circles and legal systems – basically anywhere you can think of!

Social conditioning isn't a bad thing in and of itself. It can help us maintain a sense of order and create standards of behaviour that keep people safe and society functioning smoothly. However, it can also perpetuate inequalities, stereotypes and biases. Social conditioning can make it difficult to challenge the dominant 'narratives' or stories in our societies. It can limit individual freedom and expression and trap us into having limiting and unrealistic beliefs and expectations of our relationships. The messages we receive differ according to race, ethnicity, culture, gender and sexuality sure, but *everyone* receives some form of social conditioning.[2] The messages we receive create a story in our mind and this story guides the choices we make and the way we engage in relationships. The story influences what we think is right and wrong, what we will tolerate and what we won't.

It might seem strange to be starting a book on relationships talking about beliefs and social conditioning but really, our beliefs and expectations about partners and relationships is where *everything* starts. In order to understand the motivations behind your relationship patterns, choices, behaviours and expectations we first need to understand the ways you have been conditioned – why you are the way you are. This chapter explores the ways in which social conditioning gives us all an unconscious 'blueprint' for how to engage in relationships.

Our beliefs and expectations about partners and relationships is where everything starts.

Let's begin by taking a look at three key areas of influence. First, your family of origin. Second, your gender. And third, your social and cultural norms. Together these make up our social blueprint. Let's start with your family of origin.

Family of origin

Your family of origin is the environment in which you were raised. It's where you came from and where you spent most of your time as a child. It might have been with your parent/s or carers, your auntie or uncle, a family friend, your grandparents or foster parents.

Your family of origin is where you first learn to make sense of the world. It shapes your earliest beliefs about relationships. How you see people engage with each other, who does what, how they communicate and what they argue about influences the relationship blueprint you create. You absorb it all, store it away and refer back to it as your 'baseline' when you are an adult in a relationship yourself.

We might have hated what we saw as children and try to do the opposite as adults. Or we might unconsciously create the same dynamic because it's very familiar to us. We do this because of something known as the 'mere-exposure effect' or 'familiarity principle'. This concept suggests we are all wired to be attracted to and feel safe with what's familiar, not necessarily what's healthy.[3] It's a bit of a pain in the neck if you ask me! And it's why a spark in the initial stages of dating is *not* a reliable way of determining what that relationship will be like down the track.

We humans are a complicated bunch and often choose people who mirror our unmet needs in childhood. We choose people who demonstrate the same deficit we experienced as a way of re-enacting that bond where we didn't get our needs met. We do this in an attempt to have these needs met in the form of an adult attachment. Now, if you have no idea what I am talking about when I say 'attachment' don't worry because the next chapter explains 'attachment theory' in detail.[4]

Imagine for a moment growing up in a family where your parents bickered constantly. You saw them getting annoyed and frustrated with one another every other day. Your mother would come and tell you all about your father and how wrong he was to have done what he did. She made you feel like you had to take sides. You felt conflicted. Being a kind and compassionate kid, you learned to help, to care for the emotions of others and to soothe your mother when she was distressed. There's nothing wrong with that!

The problems start later, when, as an adult, you might struggle with boundaries. It's no surprise because they were never modelled to you as a child. You might struggle with people-pleasing and self-sacrificing – giving up your wants and needs to tend to the needs of others – because you had to put your needs aside to comfort your mother. You might think it's normal to be in a relationship where you constantly bicker and criticise one another. You might unconsciously choose a partner with similar characteristics to your mother. You might find it difficult to communicate your needs or feel like having needs in the first place makes you 'too much'. This person might make you feel like you have to put your needs aside to comfort them. Over time, what happens is you don't feel seen or heard or fully understood. This is an example of how our family of origin primes whom we choose.

Gender

Growing up we learn how a good little boy, girl or person should behave. We learn how we should look and act in order to fit in and be loved. Most of us learn this fairly quickly because the negative reinforcement for *not* fitting those social norms can be brutal. We get teased and bullied by our peers if we are not 'girly' enough; we get pushed around and beaten up if we are not 'manly' enough. We are taught to conform to certain ideas of mas-culinity and femininity that we are told are attractive and desirable.

6

But our gender is *not* something we are born identifying with or knowing how to perform. It's something we are taught.

It's important to note here that gender and sex are different. Sex refers to biological and physiological characteristics. Gender is a social construct, and it develops through what we see, hear and experience. This development starts the moment we are born or, sometimes, even before we are born, if you count gender reveal parties!

We are constructing and confirming our gender and the gender of our children all the time without even realising it. Our clothing and toy stores are categorised into boy and girl (usually blue and pink); our bathrooms are designated male and female; the activities we choose are either masculine or feminine; even certain professions are associated with gender. We are constantly making choices influenced by our gender in most areas of our lives.

The concept of 'gender performativity' was introduced by the American philosopher and gender studies scholar Judith Butler in the 1990s. Judith suggests we act out our gender in the way we speak, walk, engage with people and dress.[5] We absorb messages about gender and those messages become our internal reality. We then express our internal reality and gender identity through our choices, actions and behaviour. Essentially, we *perform* our gender. You might be thinking, 'Okay, but how is this relevant to relationships?' Well, the gender roles we abide by and what we see modelled influence the beliefs we have about relationships.

Let's think for a moment about gender and the role it plays in dating. Growing up, we are filled with ideas about how we should behave according to our pronoun. Heteronormative culture (viewing heterosexuality as the norm) is largely responsible for this.

When it comes to dating, men typically receive the message that they have to be the one to pursue, and that doing so is assertive. Women typically receive the message they should wait to be pursued because if they pursue they'll seem desperate or domineering. Men receive the message they have to be able to provide for a family, while women receive the message they should be soft and nurturing. Men receive the message they shouldn't be too emotional, while women expressing emotions are seen as 'too much'.

It doesn't make sense. These bizarre contradictions make a lot of people unhappy. Everyone is playing a role trying to be who they *think* they're supposed to be, but to please whom exactly? Who made these rules anyway?

We first learn about gender roles in our family of origin. The main female role model influences how you perceive femininity and the main male role model influences how you perceive masculinity. These role models may not have been your parents, they might have been any influential person in your life of either gender.

Things are changing now, but most of us will have grown up with people displaying binary and heteronormative expressions of gender. This can be limiting, especially for those who don't feel they fit into this binary model.

Social and cultural norms

Our beliefs around marriage and monogamy are good examples of the influence of social and cultural norms. In the West many of us are focused on autonomous marriages for love, however, in a lot of cultures consensual arranged marriages are considered the norm. I am not saying either is right or wrong, just that whichever option you grew up with will likely form part of your beliefs. If you grew up in the US in a culture focused on individual freedom, personal rights and a romanticised view of marriage, you may feel uncomfortable with the concept of arranged marriages. If you grew up in the East, especially in countries like India where arranged marriages are common, you might not think twice about it. In fact, you might even have some judgements about the West's obsession with marrying for love!

That's how social and cultural norms influence our beliefs and what we perceive to be right and wrong, acceptable and unacceptable, and good and bad. There are so many rules, beliefs and norms that influence our attitudes towards relationships. Many people believe in finding a 'forever person', or that divorce is wrong, or that you should stay together for the sake of the children even if the relationship is terrible. These rigid beliefs can paralyse people. They reinforce the idea that relationships are binary in nature when really they are far more nuanced.

Such messages are prominent in our culture and are unhelpful. They suggest that we must search for unconditional love, and that we are not complete without a partner, when the reality is that all adult relationships are conditional. We are told to preserve the relationship at all costs but what if the relationship is unhealthy? What if it doesn't serve our best interests anymore? What if it's served its purpose?

Staying in a relationship that is not right for us can inhibit our personal growth, limit our ability to achieve our dreams – and make us wildly unhappy. And for what? Who benefits? Relationships make valuable contributions to our lives regardless of their length because, after all, the measure of success is not length but growth.

Values

Your personal values develop through the experiences you have with your family of origin, society and culture. They are informed by your beliefs and education. They guide your behaviour as they act as motivators.[6] The difference between beliefs and values is that your beliefs are a set of ideas you hold to be true about the world around you. Your values on the other hand are the guiding principles for living your life, engaging with the world and demonstrating what is important to you.

Personal values act like a compass. When you are living in alignment with your values it's like you are facing your true north and you feel good. When you are acting in ways that go against your values it can lead to feelings of guilt and shame. This is why it's important to understand your values.

You might value honesty which means you try to act and communicate in a way that is open and transparent. You might value open-mindedness which leads you to try to accept others who are different from you rather than judging them.

Your values influence not only how you show up in your relationships and the sort of partner you are, but also what you expect from others.

Relationships in the modern age

The ideas we have around what a successful relationship – and a successful life – look like are finally changing. Many of us grew up with an image of success that went along these lines . . . finish school, get a good job, find a partner, settle down, buy a house, get a pet and have a kid or two. While there is nothing wrong with this path *if* this is what success looks like to you, it is a pretty narrow path for an entire species.

What about those who don't want to buy a house and would prefer to travel? What about those who don't want to have children? What about those who don't want to get married? What about those who want to be polyamorous? What about those who are asexual and want a committed relationship without sexual intimacy? Where does this limited version of 'success' leave them?

We live in a time when the structures of relationships are morphing every day. It is a time of choice. We can choose whom we want to be in a relationship with, how we want that relationship to evolve and how long we want to stay in it. We can do this by aligning our relationship-based decisions with our values and challenging old outdated beliefs that no longer serve.

While your beliefs may have been conditioned and mostly unconscious, now you can choose what you agree with, what you want to challenge, and what you want to unlearn. The beliefs you have about relationships, about gender roles and about what you expect from a partner may have been mostly unconscious . . . until now. It's time to ask yourself what still aligns with who you are and what doesn't.

This was incredibly important for me as someone who came out later in life. Part of the process of exploring my sexuality was the realisation that most of my beliefs about relationships were heteronormative. I realised I had very gendered expectations after I started dating people who were *not* cis men. I had beliefs about who should ask whom out, who should pay, who should text and when, the list goes on and on. These expectations no longer worked for me so I did exactly what I am asking you to do now: stop, reflect and ask yourself what do I want to keep, what do I want to challenge and what do I want to unlearn?

Choosing your beliefs is a powerful process and is tied to living your values. It helps us to explore how we want to show up in the world, who we want to be, how we want to behave and how we treat others. It's your choice. You are an adult and you are no longer defined by the beliefs and values of your parents or care-givers. You are free to choose who you want to be and how you want to live your life.

Summary

- We are all socially conditioned from the moment we come into this world; trained to think, feel and behave in certain ways depending on what is considered acceptable and unacceptable within our culture and society. Our family of origin creates the blueprint for our relationship structures.

- Social conditioning influences our beliefs and values and is further ingrained through positive and negative reinforcement.

- The way we 'perform' our gender includes how we show up in the world and how we engage in our relationships.

- Social and cultural norms prescribe the relationship structures we perceive to be normal, and what we think is right and wrong. This creates binary views about how relationships should be.

- We have the opportunity as adults to choose what we believe, what we value and how we will engage in relationships. You can accept, challenge or unlearn beliefs. You can change the ones that no longer serve you, and honour those that do.

Activity: Challenging beliefs

It's time to explore the beliefs you hold about relationships, where they come from and what you want to challenge or unlearn. Have a think about the following questions:

Family of origin

- How has your family of origin shaped your beliefs about relationships?
- How would you describe the most prominent relationship you saw growing up?

Gender

- What beliefs do you have about how relationships should be according to your gender?
- What did you learn about being a man or a woman from the most important role models in your life? What did you learn about masculine and feminine roles from these people?
- How do you perform your gender? If you are in a relationship, how does your partner perform their gender?
- What roles and responsibilities do you take on yourself or expect of a partner based on gender?

Social and cultural norms

- What beliefs do you have about how relationships 'should' be?
- How does this affect how you engage in romantic relationships?

Values

- What are your personal values?
- What do you value in a partner and/or a relationship?

Accept, challenge or unlearn

- Which of these beliefs do you still agree with?
- Which beliefs do you want to challenge?
- Which beliefs are you now choosing to unlearn?

2

Drivers

What drives how you engage in relationships?

We all have baggage. We all enter relationships with wounds from past hurts, patterns of how we engage, and expectations we think should be common sense (but aren't). We all have ideas about how a partner should behave and treat us which then become unravelled when they fail to meet these expectations.

Most of us are unaware of exactly what drives us. This is because our relationship drivers are developed in childhood. They start with the most formative connection; the relationship with our parents or caregivers. The way our parents or caregivers responded to our emotional needs and whether we felt safe, loved and nurtured, influences how we show up in our adult relationships. The type of bond we experienced with our parents or caregivers guides the type of partnership we desire in adult love. This is called attachment.

'Attachment theory' has become very popular in recent years thanks in part to TikTok and Instagram! While it's by no means the only theory, it does offer a helpful framework to start exploring how you engage in relationships. Well before social media, the theory was first developed by the British psychiatrist John Bowlby. Essentially, it refers to the type of bond that developed between you and your parent or carer in childhood.[1] As a child, you developed an attachment style based on the way your parents or caregivers responded to your emotional needs. If they were responsive most of the time, then you likely developed 'secure attachment'. If they were inconsistent – or worse – then it's likely you developed 'insecure attachment'.

The way our parents or caregivers responded to our emotional needs and whether we felt safe, loved and nurtured, influences how we show up in our adult relationships.

According to the theory, there is one type of secure attachment but *three* types of insecure attachment: anxious, avoidant and disorganised. The thing to remember is that we develop these attachment styles, or 'traits' as I like to call them, out of *necessity*. It is not a choice. These traits are coping strategies and come from the ways we adapt to get our needs met. Babies rely on their parents or caregivers for survival. If we sense they are unable to care for us in the ways we need, we perceive it as a threat to our safety and we develop ways of coping in order to survive.

Attachment theory can help you to understand your own coping strategies or traits. It can help you learn to respond to your needs and better understand the needs and coping strategies of your partner/s. In this chapter we'll explore attachment theory and how your attachment style influences your wants, needs, and the way you engage in relationships.

Let's delve into the attachment styles. While reading the following section, have a think about which style you most identify with. You might find you relate to more than one. If so, that's perfectly normal. Sometimes different relationships bring out different sides of us. Just try to see which traits you relate most to when you're stressed, because it's in those times that we see our attachment traits most clearly.

Note: I am going to use the term 'parent' regularly throughout this chapter but your primary attachment figure might very well have been a grandparent, carer, foster parent, uncle or aunt. It's basically the main person or people who raised you. I am just using the term 'parent' for simplicity.

Secure attachment

Scenario: You grew up in a household where the family was seen as important. You remember playing with both your dads in the garden in the summer, they helped you with your homework when you struggled and they encouraged you to try new things. They weren't overbearing but you always knew if you needed them, they would be there. You had dinner together most nights and they were interested in how school was going. On days when you had issues with friends at school, coming home felt like a relief. Even though your parents never got involved, they were there for you. They held you when you cried about being bullied and let you know you always belonged with them.

As you got older, you built solid relationships with friends and later with partners. Your parents treated you well and that gave you a good base for what to expect from a partner and how to show up in a relationship. You always saw them treat each other with respect even if they did argue at times. Later, you were able to negotiate and set boundaries with them. They respected your individuality and autonomy.

As an adult, you feel comfortable in your skin most of the time and know you have a lot to offer. In relationships, you are good at sharing your emotions, wants and needs. You are okay with managing conflict – it's never easy but it's doable – and you tend to have stable relationships.

—

If your emotional needs were met by your parents *most of the time* this is known as 'secure attachment'. Basically, they provided a *secure base* for you.[2] [3] It's likely you felt your relationship was important, they paid attention to you and engaged with you when you were upset. They listened to you when you faced challenges and helped you find solutions. You knew you could rely on them. They were consistent and you felt protected and safe in the family unit. A secure base gives you a feeling of safety and security stemming from the primary attachment relationship. It gives you the confidence to go out and explore, try new things and just be a kid.

When you've had secure attachment you grow into an adult who tends to have positive relationships with others. You're likely to have good self-esteem and self-efficacy most of the time, are comfortable hanging out with different groups of people, and are easy to get along with. You are comfortable spending time both alone and in company and have good emotional intelligence and emotional awareness.

People with secure traits tend not to feel a lot of anxiety about their relationships. They're good at shifting between alone time and time with their partner/s as well as adapting to change and managing conflict. The key words to remember here are – *most of the time*. No-one shows up like this all the time because we all have triggers and get stressed and overwhelmed. The statistic varies a lot when it comes to what percentage of the population experiences what style. Most studies suggest anywhere from 53 to 66 per cent of people in the West are securely attached.[4] [5]

Insecure attachment: anxious, avoidant and disorganised

Anxious (also known as preoccupied)

Scenario: You grew up with two brothers and you were the middle child. There was a significant age gap between you and your brothers. You were raised by your mum and while she was around and available, she was inconsistent with her love and affection and often seemed to favour your brothers. Sometimes she would be very affectionate and complimentary but when she was stressed you felt like you were a burden. She didn't say it, but you could sense it. Her mood seemed to change and she would get short with you. She worked so hard to support you and your brothers and you knew it was a lot for her to manage. You didn't want to be a burden so you kept your feelings and needs to yourself.

You try to be helpful and show you appreciate her. Sometimes it works, but sometimes it doesn't. There is no rhyme or reason to when she is loving and when she is annoyed. Maybe it's just stress?

As you got older, you learned to be hyperaware of your environment and the people around you. You work extra hard to prove that you are worthy of love and have a deep fear of rejection. In relationships, you tend to over-function and attract unpredictable people. You try to earn their love and acceptance and find yourself constantly anxious and seeking their approval and validation.

21

You're afraid of being seen as 'too much' or 'too needy' so you try to hide it.

—

If you developed anxious attachment as a child it is often because you had a parent or caregiver who responded to your emotional needs in an inconsistent or unreliable way. They might have been dealing with their own challenges and therefore weren't able to give you the consistency and stability you required.

This meant you didn't know when your needs would be met. They might have responded openly and warmly to you sometimes and then seemed annoyed with you at others. You didn't know what to expect and this resulted in feelings of insecurity and rejection. You might have learned to read people's behaviour and even manage their emotional states because you had to do this with your parent.

As an adult, anxious attachment might result in you wanting a lot of validation from your partner/s. Dating might be difficult because it sparks the feeling of anxiety you experienced in childhood. You might seek commitment quickly to ease your anxiety or want a lot of contact including lots of texting and calling. You might become highly focused on your partner/s, their needs and whether they like you, rather than tuning in and exploring if you really like them.

When it comes to navigating issues, you might prefer to talk things through and unpack issues out loud as soon as possible because you emotionally regulate through others rather than on your own. Separation and time apart might be quite difficult and you might find yourself feeling jealous and insecure, questioning the relationship and the security of the bond for no apparent reason.

Avoidant (also known as dismissive)

Scenario: You don't remember much from your childhood. At age two your mother died of cancer and your dad struggled to cope. You were lucky that he was able to hire a nice lady to work as a nanny until you went to school but he wasn't really around. You felt alone, like no-one cared for you. You spent a lot of time by yourself. Things weren't necessarily that bad, but you didn't feel you had anyone to rely on, anyone who supported you. You felt alone in the world. You built walls to protect yourself.

You don't need anyone now. The people you date tell you they find it hard to get close to you, that you pull away and seem distant. You become emotionally overwhelmed by their need for connection and find them smothering. It's very unattractive. Why can't they be as independent as you? This results in you having relationships where you feel like something is missing but you don't realise it's because of your emotional blocks. It results in a deep sense of shame. You keep trying with new people but the issue remains. You end up hurting people because you pull away when they want more. It's not intentional, it's self-preservation. It's a constant dance between the desire to connect and protect.

—

If you have avoidant attachment it is likely because your emotional needs were not met as a child. Your parent may have been absent a lot, dealing with their own issues, or emotionally unavailable. Whatever the reason, they were unable to meet your emotional needs. This led to you learning how to self-soothe at a young age and erect emotional walls to protect yourself. You likely spent a fair bit of time either alone, or in your own imagination. You had to become self-sufficient much earlier than you should have and didn't feel like you could rely on anyone for anything. Performance and achievement were likely important in your household.

As an adult, this resulted in your being very self-reliant. You might struggle to let people in emotionally, to rely on others or even to trust people. You might find it difficult to commit to relationships because they affect your autonomy. You might feel like others need too much from you and find this smothering and unattractive. You might need a lot of alone time to recharge after spending time with people. You might find it difficult to ask for what you need, or even know what you need. You might be disconnected from your emotions and find your sense of self is highly connected with external achievements and profes-sional roles. It might be difficult for you communicate in times of conflict. As a result, you shut down and emotionally distance yourself.

Disorganised (also known as fearful avoidant)

Scenario: You grew up with a mother who used drugs. Your dad left when you were young. You never knew him but sometimes you wished he would turn up and save you. Your mum had many different partners but the relationships never lasted. When she was single she was okay, but when her partners were around it was like you didn't exist. Sometimes, when she was drunk, she'd get angry and take it out on you.

As an adult you don't blame your mother because now you know how bad her own childhood was. Still, you can't seem to move past the pattern that was created for you. You date people who have substance abuse problems, or who are controlling, or whose mental health is not being managed. It starts out well and then it slowly comes apart and they end up treating you exactly like your mum did. You want love, you want to feel safe and secure but for some reason that experience eludes you. The minute it feels okay, something happens and it all goes to shit. You break up and get back together, again and again and it's no better now than it was the first time.

—

Disorganised attachment forms when the person who is responsible for caring for you is also a source of fear. Growing up in a household where your parent hurt you can be incredibly confusing and damaging. Your parent may have struggled with addiction or mental health issues or may have been abusive. This results in your attachment becoming disorganised because love, safety and fear are mixed up.

As an adult, people with disorganised attachment often have deep-seated fears when it comes to intimacy. They want closeness, but it also scares them because they associate it with being hurt, so they end up in a 'push-pull' dynamic. You might swing between love and wanting closeness so you pull close, but also fear, so you push away. Again, it's the dance between the desire to connect and protect. You might fear rejection and then self-sabotage. If you hurt yourself, others can't hurt you. You might find yourself being controlling or insensitive towards your partner/s out of fear. You might be prone to using drugs or alcohol to cope and self-soothe in times of distress.

—

Do you see yourself in any of these attachment styles? If you relate to one of the insecure styles, I want to take a moment and stress that *there is nothing wrong with you*. The traits we develop in childhood are a result of trying to cope with our environment and get our needs met. Again, it's not a choice. There is often shame and judgement attached to the ways these traits are exhibited in adulthood which just perpetuates the idea that there is something 'wrong' with you.

In this book you'll find tools and strategies not only to support you to better manage how your attachment shows up but also to help you regulate your emotions and manage conflict. So don't get down on yourself if you relate to the insecure styles.

The traits we develop in childhood are a result of trying to cope with our environment and get our needs met.

I am a therapist and I am primarily avoidant! The scenario in the avoidant section was my story. That was me in my twenties. I have done a lot of work on my attachment style and how the traits show up in my life and relationships so while I no longer engage the way I described, I certainly did before I learned about this stuff. We are all human, and learning about our patterns of behaviour is the first step to changing them.

I also want to acknowledge that different people bring out different sides of us so while you might have one predominant style, you might also have traits from the others. If, for example, you identify with more of the anxious tendencies but are in a relationship with someone who exhibits more secure traits, you might feel more secure. Or if you are with someone who exhibits more anxious traits, you might find yourself being a bit more avoidant. How these traits show up changes as we grow and is influenced by the traits of our partner/s. We might also show up differently depending on the relationship whether it be a friendship, a casual dating experience or a long-term romantic relationship. Once you have identified your attachment style, you can then explore how this shows up through your behaviour.

There are two attachment-related dynamics that I often see people get stuck in. They are 'attachment protest behaviours' and the 'pursuer/distancer dynamic'.[6] Let's explore both of these.

Attachment protest behaviours

Imagine you have a little baby. Let's say they're one year old. You're sitting with them in the living room, they are in a highchair and you are feeding them some mango. Your phone starts ringing. It's your partner and you answer it and get into a conversation about what you're going to have for dinner. Your baby notices you are no longer paying attention so they start to point at things, hoping your gaze will follow their finger and you will re-engage. You miss this attempt at connection.

Your baby then throws a piece of mango on the floor, again trying to get your attention. Finally they become frustrated and start hitting the table on the high chair, screaming and crying until you tell your partner you've got to go, put the phone down and re-engage. They finally settle as they are feeling connected to you.

This is what we call 'attachment protest'. Attachment protest behaviours are behaviours that demand reconnection through exaggerated expressions. They stem from a fear of separation and abandonment.[7] We see it play out in a similar way in adult relationships and even with pets. Does anyone else's cat get louder and more intense until she gets what she wants or is it just mine?

Let's imagine how this plays out in an adult relationship between Noah (they) and Lily (she). Noah has some anxious tendencies and likes to feel close and connected to Lily. Noah likes spending time together and can really feel it when Lily is distracted and not emotionally present. Lily has been stressed with work recently and every time they're together Noah feels like Lily is distant, has a wall up and is not really present.

This makes Noah anxious. Noah starts wondering if Lily is questioning the relationship and needs reassurance. Noah worries that asking this directly may get a bad reaction because Lily is already stressed. Noah goes about getting this validation in other ways like texting Lily more often, hoping to get validation through her responses. Noah ends up becoming more worried as Lily is rubbish at texting, especially when stressed. Noah then starts giving Lily the silent treatment and being passive-aggressive, but worse still, Lily doesn't notice.

Finally, Noah becomes overwhelmed and starts to act out towards Lily by being very critical and displaying big emotions when Lily arrives home from work. Lily is shocked. She doesn't understand what brought this on because she thought everything was fine. She had missed Noah's more subtle attempts to connect and only realised how Noah was feeling when they became upset and angry. It looks like Noah went from zero to a hundred which we know they didn't. The challenge is Noah did not tell Lily how they were feeling.

—

Do you see the similarity between Noah and the baby? Both are trying to get their needs met but Noah struggled to do so in a healthy way so resorted to 'protest behaviours'.[8] It's not that protest behaviours are always unhealthy and should be avoided at all costs. Some are just our learned responses. The point is that while they are effective in childhood, they are not effective now. No-one likes being on the receiving end of an adult tantrum! These sorts of emotional expressions are understandable from children who haven't yet learned to regulate their emotions but as adults it's up to us to learn how to communicate our needs not only for our own mental health and wellness but also for our partner/s'.

The pursuer/distancer (or withdrawer) dynamic

I see this dynamic regularly. It refers to the pattern of one partner seeking closeness and connection (the pursuer), and the other being prone to distance and withdrawal (the distancer or withdrawer). It's an example of the challenge in a relationship between someone with anxious tendencies and someone with more avoidant tendencies. But it goes further than that. It's present in most relationships. It represents the constant dance between the desire for togetherness and separateness or connection and freedom. The person more prone to anxiety seeks out closeness, validation and prioritises the partnership, while the person more prone to avoidance needs their independence and space, which results in them distancing or withdrawing when they feel their partner trying to get too close. This creates what's known as the 'pursuer/distancer' dynamic.

It's a constant dance between the desire for togetherness and separateness.

It's a double-edged sword where no-one knows what happened first. Did the distancer pull back resulting in the pursuer feeling the disconnection and pulling closer? Or did the pursuer pull closer resulting in the distancer feeling overwhelmed and then pushing back and withdrawing? Whatever the case, it's a common pattern which, although potentially distressing, can be overcome. We'll explore how to navigate this dynamic in later chapters.

Attachment and partner choice

Your attachment style influences the partners you choose and whom you feel comfortable with. It also influences the sorts of challenges you have in relationships.

Let's start with the secure attachment style. People with secure attachment tend to be more likely to be in long-term relationships with other secure people. This is because we are wired to be attracted to what is familiar. People with secure attachment tend to be aware of their needs, have good levels of self-esteem and are comfortable being relied upon by their partners. They tend to be attracted to people who have similar traits because that's what they know. It makes them more likely to walk away from relationships where their needs are not being met and/or they are not being treated well.

The difference between secure and insecure attachments is when a secure person might walk away, someone with insecure attachment might be drawn in because that inconsistency is familiar to them. They may be used to their needs not being met, not feeling good enough or being treated poorly because that's what happened in childhood. Maybe they had to fight to be heard, maybe they were used to being criticised, maybe they were used to having to prove themselves. These early experiences create a blueprint for what we expect from our partner/s, how we believe things should be in a relationship, what we think we deserve and also what we are attracted to and feel comfortable with.

Some myths I often hear when it comes to attachment are that anxious and avoidant people cannot work together, that everyone should seek a secure partner and that disorganised attachment is always going to be an issue. I want to be very clear – this is bullshit.

Let's debunk these myths. First, couples with one anxious and one avoidant partner absolutely can have a loving relationship.

Your attachment style is made up of a set of learned coping strategies, it's not your character or personality. *You* are not secure, anxious, avoidant or disorganised – you just have those traits.

Attachment is a framework to help you better understand yourself, your needs and how you relate to others. That said, it is up to you to use the information to your benefit. Sure, if you have a couple with anxious and avoidant tendencies who have a total lack of self-awareness and refuse to do the work to better understand themselves and each other then yes, it can make for a very difficult dynamic. However, if there is a *willingness* to learn about themselves, to work on their attachment traits, and to truly show up, then it *can* work.

Second, choosing someone based on their attachment style – which is difficult to do anyway because you don't often see their true style until well into the dating process – misses so many of the other important things to look for in a partner. Do you have similar values? Are they considerate? Do you respect them? Are they a good person? Being securely attached says almost nothing about their personality or character.

Finally, people with disorganised attachment can heal and work through their attachment wounds like anyone else. They may have extra work to do in order to dismantle the connection of love and fear that was established early on, but it can be done. People healing from disorganised attachment can be incredible partners.

Put simply, it's not so much your attachment style per se that determines the relationships you have, but rather what you do with it.

Connection and protection

Attachment is a binary concept and may not resonate with you. Its universality is often challenged due to the differences in parenting across cultures. It may seem too rigid or you may notice yourself in various styles, which can be confusing. What I find helpful is to simplify it and instead explore the dance between 'connection and protection'.

This dance happens within all of us, regardless of our attachment style. Our dance is demonstrated through the steps we take towards connection and how we try to protect ourselves. What your dance looks like will often be guided by your early experiences, wounds, trauma, and relational challenges. While part of us deeply wants connection, another part doesn't feel safe because in the past connection has led to being deeply hurt. This then activates another part of us focused on protection. This is why we have that push and pull between:

- I want you close but not *too* close.
- I want to feel connected but I am afraid so I push you away.
- I want you to know me, but I won't open up and feel vulnerable.
- I want you to make me a priority, but I don't want to come across as needy so I don't communicate my needs.

This back and forth is an internal conflict between what we really want – connection – and also our deep need to feel safe and therefore to protect. While this may be more pronounced for those who have experienced trauma or been in unhealthy relationships, this dance can happen to anyone and everyone.

This is why it is helpful to explore what the dance between connection and protection looks like for you. How do you try to connect? And in what ways do you try to protect yourself? In your childhood, were you trying to protect yourself from a feeling of disconnection and abandonment? From abuse? From trauma? From feeling overwhelmed and suffocated? The dance between connection and protection is something that plays out in all of our relational and dating experiences, but the ways that we try to connect or protect will differ.

If you can understand the ways that you try to connect and the triggers that lead you to go into protection mode, then it will help you navigate how you relate to others. The reality is most of our unhelpful traits or behaviours in dating come from a desire to protect ourselves. They are coping strategies that we learned when we didn't necessarily have the brain development or awareness to come up with better strategies. It's why we need to be gentle with ourselves. The younger parts of us did the best that they could to protect us. The trouble is, the ways we protected ourselves as children can become barriers to getting the connection we want as adults. This is why we need to understand our dance, lean in, self-soothe and choose new ways to show up and navigate the dance between connection and protection.

You are a secure base

You can heal attachment wounds by creating a secure base both within yourself and with others. We develop a secure base in childhood by having a parent or caregiver who is attuned to our emotional needs, displays warmth and kindness, is supportive and encouraging, and allows us to express ourselves free from judgement. These same traits and qualities are how we start to heal our own attachment and create a secure base within ourselves. The second part of the book will explore how to do this with your partner/s or future partner/s, but for now we'll look at how to achieve a secure base within yourself.

First, you need to start giving yourself the love, acceptance, care, kindness and support you needed as a child but didn't receive. This might mean treating yourself like someone you are responsible for or someone you love deeply. Think of the person you are most kind, supportive and generous towards. How do you talk to them? How do you treat them? How do you support them? Now, how would it feel to treat yourself that way?

Creating a secure base involves connecting with your emotions and allowing yourself to be vulnerable. It involves exploring your fears and learning where they come from. It involves embracing your wants and needs as well as communicating them. It involves learning to regulate your emotions and set boundaries with yourself and others. Creating a secure base means learning to trust yourself by slowing tuning in and acting on your gut. It's not easy, but it's worth it.

Your healing journey will be different depending on your predominant attachment style. It might involve you letting your walls down and opening up if you lean towards avoidance, or learning to open up and trust if you lean towards disorganised traits. Wherever you are starting from, the journey is about leaning into and meeting your emotional needs. It's about supporting yourself like the secure parent many of us wished we had.

This process of developing self-awareness is one of the *most* important steps. How can we improve if we are not able to reflect upon our own behaviours, coping strategies and tendencies and really think about where they come from? How can we respond to partners in healthy, constructive and loving ways if we are not open to receiving feedback ourselves? And how can we improve if we are not willing to take ownership?

Of course, attachment is not the only thing to consider when it comes to dating and relationships. There are many other ingredients that are essential for creating safe love.

Summary

- Your attachment style is determined by the way your parents or caregivers responded to your emotional needs in childhood.

- 'Attachment theory' helps us understand the way we relate to partners and our automatic coping/self-soothing strategies.

- There is one type of secure attachment and three types of insecure attachment – anxious, avoidant and disorganised.

- Your attachment style creates a blueprint for what you expect from a partner, how you believe things should be in relationships, and also whom you are attracted to and feel comfortable with.

- We all dance between the desire to connect and protect. This back and forth is an internal conflict between what we really want – connection – and also our deep need to feel safe and therefore to protect ourselves from pain.

Activity

Have a think and answer the following questions:

- How do you remember feeling as a child in your family of origin? When you recall your childhood what is the strongest feeling or memory?

- What attachment style do you relate to most?

- How does your attachment style show up in the way you engage in your adult relationships?

- Do you have any coping styles or behaviours that may have helped you as a child that now have a negative effect on your relationships? If yes, what could you do differently now?

- Do you have a certain attachment style you tend to attract in partners? If so, how does that dynamic usually look?

- Are there any attachment traits that have been particularly problematic in your relationships?

- What are three things you can commit to doing that will support the journey towards creating a more secure base within yourself?

3
Safe Love

The essential ingredients for safe love

Many of us didn't grow up with a secure base or a model for safe and loving relationships. We didn't see what safe love looked like or learn what it felt like. In writing this book, I looked back upon my Instagram posts. I wanted to know what topics resonated most with people, what they wanted to learn and where they struggled. I realised over the last two years, the posts that gained the most reach and had the most interactions were those on safe love. People wanted to know what it felt like, how to create it and, most importantly, how to be a safe partner. They also wanted to know how to identify *unsafe* love, and what to do about it.

While the criteria for healthy relationships may vary according to the type of structure you choose and the agreements you have, the components of safe love are more basic. They are the foundations on which most relationships are formed. In this chapter we'll examine what safe love feels like and what makes you a safe partner. We'll also look at what can make relationships feel unsafe. My hope is this understanding will support you to create and sustain safe, loving connections.

When I say 'safe love' I am referring to love that feels secure, respectful, supportive, consistent and stable. You can rely on one another, you are comfortable being close and intimate; you feel accepted, considered and at ease being yourself. You respond to one another's emotional needs. When there is conflict, it's handled respectfully and you're able to repair and re-establish connection. Safe love is a space where the connection is important as is your independence and freedom. It's emotionally, physically, sexually, spiritually and intellectually safe.

Safety is the single most important factor in any relationship, whether that be the relationship with yourself or with another. Safe and healthy love allows you to be yourself while also encouraging your growth. It supports your healing and helps you know yourself more deeply, allowing you to look at your patterns and unproductive coping strategies. This is because safe love – along with the right tools – allows you to soften, let your walls down and stop focusing so hard on protecting yourself.

Safe love provides a sense of comfort, a feeling of security, a 'knowing' in your body. It's like a protected place you can return to where you're able to soften and be yourself. In safe relationships you're able to:

- Communicate your needs and boundaries openly and have them accepted, acknowledged and respected. That may not mean every single need is met, but it does mean you're able to express your needs and be respected.
- Communicate when things upset you, offer feedback and hold one another accountable in a loving way. That doesn't mean

communication will always be perfect, but it does mean you work towards maintaining respectful communication.

- Maintain a sense of connection and emotional responsiveness to one another. That doesn't mean you'll never have periods of disconnection or face challenges, but it does mean you value and prioritise reconnection.
- Be vulnerable and express how you feel. That doesn't mean you will always agree on everything, but it does mean they will accept and respect how you feel.
- Be loved and accepted for who you are. It doesn't mean there won't be things you need to work on and improve, but you will not have to hide fundamental parts of who you are to be loved.

Does this sound a bit too good to be true? I'm not saying there are never issues or challenges in safe, loving relationships; of course there are. I don't want to paint an unrealistic picture here so let me be very plain. What sets safe love apart is not the absence of issues or challenges, but rather how those issues are dealt with. In safe love, you will still have arguments, conflicts, periods of disconnection, times where you frustrate one another, times where you hurt or upset one another. You will make mistakes that damage the connection. The difference in safe love is that these challenges are navigated with respect, care, consideration and a willingness to take accountability and restore the connection.

Creating safe love doesn't just happen. It's an *active* process. It is something that we co-create together.

Creating safe love doesn't just happen. It's an *active* process. It is something that we co-create together and it takes time, commitment and care. It's not just about *finding* a safe partner, it's about *being* a safe partner because we need *both* elements to create a safe relationship.

Safe love starts with you

Creating a safe and loving relationship starts with the most important relationship you will ever have; your relationship with yourself. It starts with you showing up for yourself in a safe and supportive way because this helps you identify what safe love feels like with another.

I am not saying you have to love yourself *before* you can love someone else or that you have to be fully healed. Sometimes a safe and loving relationship with another is the catalyst for improving your relationship with yourself. What I am saying is how you treat yourself and the relationship you have with yourself informs what you accept from others. When you have a good relationship with yourself, it sets the standard for what you'll accept from others. When you have a poor relationship with yourself, you may be more prone to accepting that kind of treatment from others. This is why before we jump into how to create a safe and loving relationship with partner/s, we'll explore how to create a safe, loving and supportive relationship with yourself!

When you have a good relationship with yourself, it sets the standard for what you accept from others.

In a perfect world, we would all have had safe love modelled to us by our parents or caregivers. They would have shown us how to love and care for ourselves and helped us build our self-worth and self-esteem. This would have acted as a base upon which we build our relationship with others. That's what happens when we have a 'secure base' in childhood and our emotional needs are met.[1] [2] Unfortunately, as we explored in the last chapter, many of us did not have that experience. We didn't learn how to create a healthy relationship with ourselves or with others, so part of creating a better relationship with yourself involves what we therapists call 'reparenting'. That means showing up for yourself in a way that you wished your parents or caregivers might have. It means being the parent you may have always wanted and needed. It means meeting your emotional and physical needs and giving yourself the love and care you hoped to receive as a child.

Here's how we do it.

Building a better relationship with yourself

Building a better relationship with yourself involves doing the following:

1. **Exploring, validating and responding to your needs.** Having needs doesn't make you needy, it makes you human. If you are someone who struggles to identify or communicate your needs, or feels needy for having them in the first place, then this step is incredibly important. Exploring your needs (emotional and physical), validating them and learning to respond to them is how you show up for yourself. It builds self-reliance, self-trust and helps you to know yourself more deeply. It's about showing up for yourself in the way that maybe you wished someone had shown up for you as a child.

2. **Deepening your self-awareness.** This involves being curious about your wants, needs, emotions, feelings and thoughts. It's a process of learning about yourself and paying attention to how you feel and why you feel the way you do – without judgement.

The more mindful we can be, the more conscious we become of the things that drive our thoughts, feelings and behaviours.

3. **Building self-trust.** Building trust in yourself involves making and keeping promises to yourself, acting in ways that align with your values, tuning in and listening to yourself, and having your own back. You can do this by making small, achievable commitments to yourself each day.

4. **Improving your emotional regulation.** This might involve reflecting on the things that activate or trigger you. It might mean learning to self-soothe when you're feeling stressed and learning how to respond when you're feeling overwhelmed. More on this in the next chapter.

5. **Accepting yourself for who you are.** This means giving yourself the freedom to be you, to accept who you are with all your perceived flaws and to know that regardless of what anyone else thinks or says . . . you are enough, just as you are.

6. **Being kind to yourself.** This means learning to speak to yourself like you would speak to someone you love. It means becoming mindful of your thoughts about yourself, the things you say about yourself and the beliefs that drive the way you see yourself.

7. **Letting more joy in.** Most of us need more joy and play in our lives! We need to give ourselves the opportunity to engage in activities that bring us joy and spend time doing things with no outcome in mind.

8. **Getting curious about your wounds.** This means learning about any wounds you are still carrying from childhood or past relationships and how they show up for you then doing the work to process, heal and move forward.

9. **Holding yourself accountable.** While this one is the least fun, it is necessary. A big part of any safe relationship is the willingness to take accountability for the mistakes we make,

our choices and behaviour and commit to making change when needed.

10. **Treating yourself with respect.** I put this one last because I find it's the one most people struggle with. It brings all the prior steps together and requires you to see and value yourself enough to set boundaries, care for yourself, honour yourself, act in alignment with your values, be honest with yourself and sometimes, make very hard decisions that you do not want to make but that are in your best interests. Self-respect helps you to get yourself to bed early when you're exhausted rather than binge watching TV. It helps you to walk away from situations and people where you're not being treated well. It encourages you to make the hard decisions that you know you need to make but really don't want to.

When you slowly but consistently start to show up for yourself in this way, you will notice your relationship with yourself improves. I am not saying it's easy, it's not, it can be incredibly hard at times, but so is having a poor relationship with yourself! Doing the work is hard, not doing the work is hard . . . so, as the saying goes, choose your hard.

Doing the work is hard, not doing the work is hard . . . so, as the saying goes, choose your hard.

Doing this work often goes hand in hand with facing the things we need to heal from our past. It encourages us to examine our wounds and how they show up in our relationships through the way we think, speak, act (what we do) and behave (how we do it). This is an important part of the process because often, the shame around our perceived flaws, imperfections and wounds is the very thing keeping us stuck. Those feelings stop us from doing the work to address them. It can actually be the cause of our unhelpful behaviours.

Maybe you struggle with communication, or emotional regulation, or conflict management, or are a bit anxious or avoidant at times and this leads you to act in ways that you feel guilt or shame about. Welcome to the club. It's not about being perfect, it's about pursuing growth and healing. We *all* have baggage. We all employ unproductive coping strategies and we all have to actively work on better understanding what safe love looks like for ourselves and for our partner/s. It's not something we just *know*, it's something we *learn*, build and co-create.

Part of being a safe partner is being willing to see and address the ways we show up and engage in relationships that cause our partner/s to feel unsafe, even if we do not intend to make them feel that way. This is because the reality is most of us have at least a few unproductive ways of seeking safety, connection and getting our needs met. We often develop these strategies as children, when we didn't know any better and we craved connection from a parent or caregiver. Similar to the concept of attachment protest we discussed in the last chapter, we learned, at a vulnerable time, how to get a parent or caregiver to respond to us. We then continue to utilise that strategy as an adult even if it's unproductive.

It might be that you display big expressions of emotion in order to be heard, or threaten the relationship to make your partner/s truly understand how hurt you are. It might be that you pull away and avoid sharing how you truly feel because you fear you will be 'too much'. Or maybe you are hypervigilant to their mood shifts and seek constant reassurance. These expressions often come from a place of wanting connection and emotionally safe and responsive love, but instead they can push your partner/s away and make them feel unsafe.

One way of understanding why this happens – and what we can do differently – is by getting to know the parts of you that utilise these strategies. The concept of 'parts' comes from Internal Family Systems Therapy (IFS) developed by the American family therapist and author Dr Richard Schwartz.[3] In IFS, these strategies or responses are known as 'parts'. They are parts of you that are trying to help you, protect you or get your needs met in the best way they know how. Unfortunately, it's not always productive. Let's explore this with an example.

Cam and Dani have been together for around twelve months. Things were really good for the first eight months or so, but recently they've been having some difficulties. A pattern has started to emerge which they don't know how to navigate so they came to therapy hoping to get some support.

When they first met, Cam was really attracted to Dani's vibrant personality. Dani was affectionate and expressive. She spoke her mind, she reached out for connection regularly and made herself available to Cam. Dani on the other hand was attracted to Cam's groundedness. Cam came across as secure, she had her shit together and was really smart. Dani loved that Cam was intentional about building the connection. She had her own life but she made herself available to Dani.

At the start of the relationship, they wanted the same things, they spoke about their feelings, they moved at a pace that felt good to both of them. They felt like the connection was secure, fun and based on solid foundations. Things started to change however when Cam got really busy with work about eight months in. She became less responsive via text and wasn't available to see Dani as much as she had been previously. Dani started to feel anxious.

She wondered if something had changed. She felt Cam pull away; she felt this new distance between them.

She worried she was being too sensitive but when the anxiety refused to go away, she raised it with Cam. Cam shut it down. She said everything was fine and nothing had changed. The thing was, Dani could sense that something had, in fact, changed. It wasn't just that Cam was busy, her tone had changed in her messages, she wasn't as expressive and Dani found herself reaching out for connection again and again hoping the response would give her the sense of security she'd felt before. The problem was, the more she did this, the worse the situation became. This is where they got stuck.

Cam, who was previously very emotionally available and expressive towards Dani started to pull away and withdraw because she was overwhelmed. It wasn't intentional, she genuinely was busy. She was also starting to settle into the relationship and realised that the level of input she'd been giving up to that point wasn't sustainable. Her self-care had fallen by the wayside, she didn't get the alone time she needed and she didn't know how to communicate this to Dani.

Growing up, Cam had been raised by her foster parents who, although they did their best and raised her as their own, were not emotional people. Cam spent a lot of time alone. They rarely spoke of their feelings and Cam got very good at looking out for number one. She craves intimacy, connection and safe love, but there is also a deep fear it will be taken away. She feels smothered easily and her independence is incredibly important to her.

Dani grew up with a mother who was very critical. Her mother would often compare her to her friends and make her feel like she wasn't good enough. When Dani would express her feelings, her mother would guilt-trip her and make her feel terrible for just having feelings. Dani learned to perform for her mother, to keep her happy and to stay quiet. She became adept at reading her mother's mood and behaviour so she knew what she was in for day to day.

When Cam began to pull away Dani could sense it. She could always sense it. At first, she tried to shake it off but it became harder and harder to avoid. Dani became anxious but was afraid to communicate this to Cam. When she finally did, and Cam blew it off, this felt *exactly* like what she'd experienced in childhood. Here's how their pattern went.

Cam pulled away in order to self-soothe and maintain her independence but did not communicate what she was feeling and needing to Dani. This led to Dani thinking something was wrong. It made her anxious. Dani then communicated this to Cam, who denied it because her shame led her to feel as if Dani was being critical, which she wasn't, however this made Cam defensive. Dani then felt rejected which resulted in her becoming more expressive in an attempt to soothe her anxiety and get her needs met. She started seeking more reassurance and trying harder to 'fix' what was happening. Cam withdrew even further because she felt smothered and pressured.

And on, and on, and on we go.

They both wanted to change this pattern. They both wanted to restore the connection they'd felt and to share safe love but the reality was that Cam pulling away made Dani feel unsafe, and Dani becoming more expressive and needing more from Cam made Cam feel unsafe. In order to help them navigate this dance, we need to explore what is creating the pattern and what parts are at play.

Cam's parts: Cam had a protective part that feared losing her autonomy. It feared being smothered and so every time Dani tried to pull closer, Cam's protective part took it as a threat to her independence and made her pull away.

Dani's parts: Dani had a protective part that was trying to stop her from being abandoned or rejected so when she felt Cam pull away, her protective part made her try harder to regain connection in the form of seeking out reassurance, time together and emotional connection.

How their parts interacted: basically, their protective parts were sparring with one another. Cam felt like Dani's attempts to connect were a threat to her freedom so her protective parts made her withdraw. Dani's parts felt like Cam's need for space was a threat to the connection and triggered a fear of abandonment so her protective parts made her try harder, get louder and more expressive to re-establish the connection.

Once they knew what was happening, they were able to talk to one another, learn about one another's needs and create a connection that felt safe. Cam needed to provide more emotional responsiveness to Dani, and Dani needed to self-soothe and give Cam the space she needed, which in turn, actually helped Cam be more emotionally available.

Once they were able to understand their pattern they were then able to navigate it. They realised when Dani did (X), she was trying to get (X) need met. She hoped Cam would respond by doing (X) which would meet her need, but when Cam didn't respond that way she felt (X) instead and vice versa. Using this formula to understand their pattern allowed them to better understand what they were seeking from one another and the needs that were driving their responses. This process was developed by Dr Sue Johnson and is used in Emotionally Focused Therapy.[4]

We all have parts. Some are protective, some try to manage situations and others are more vulnerable and need protecting. These parts are trying to get our needs met, keep us safe or protect us in some way, the best way they know how, but often the ways they lead us to respond or behave are unproductive. It's like we get hijacked by these parts which are so fearful of loss, or hurt or pain that they respond as if the issue were life or death. This can then make us respond in ways that feel unsafe to others. It's a strange contradiction; it's as if the parts so deeply wanting safety with another seek it in ways that can make others feel unsafe. This then creates a dynamic where no-one feels safe! This is why it's important to get to know and understand the different parts of you. Why do they react that way? What are they trying to achieve? Let's explore the parts that seek safety in relationships and how they do it.

I want you to imagine a conflict either in your current relationship or in a relationship with a former partner. Try to pick something significant. Think back to the details of the conflict, what was happening, how it felt, and ask yourself the following questions:

- How did you feel at the time? Were there any sensations in your body?
- What parts of you were present? For example a defensive part, an angry part, an anxious part, a part that withdraws, a critical part etc.?
- What was this part's role? How was it trying to help you? Was it trying to protect you from something? If so, what?
- Was this part connected to any memories?
- What did it think would happen if it didn't make you respond in that way? For example what did the defensive part think would happen if it didn't make you defensive?
- What did it need to feel safe and be able to soften?

Once you know the parts of you that drive how you respond you can be curious about them, work with them and ultimately help them to soften so there is less of a chance of you being hijacked and more conscious in how you respond. This not only helps you create a safer and healthier relationship with yourself but it will also help you to show up as a safer partner.

Creating safe love starts with you, yes, but creating a safe relationship is a mutual effort. It requires everyone involved to be invested, do the work, look at their stuff and come to the connection with care, respect and empathy. To create safe love with another, we need to develop emotional safety. Let's explore how you can show up in a way that creates safe love, then what you need from partner/s in return.

How to be an emotionally safe partner

Being an emotionally safe partner requires you to learn the skills and tools which will allow you to show up in a way that is consistent, respectful and responsive. We need to be willing to look at ourselves, our behaviours, our responses and the parts of us that may be reacting from a place of protection unproductively. Being a safe partner is a choice. It's about choosing to do the work. It's about listening to how your partner/s feel and adjusting where necessary to help them feel safer with you. It's about creating a space where you can thrive individually and together. It's not about getting it right every single time, being perfect or fully healed. It's about being open and *willing*. So, with that in mind, where do you start?

1. **Building trust.** Trust is fundamental for safe love. It is the foundation. We build trust by keeping our word, being reliable, consistent and honest. Trust is built in the small moments. By doing what you say you'll do and keeping the agreements you make in the relationship.

2. **Improving your emotional regulation.** Learning to self-soothe and regulate your emotions when you're feeling overwhelmed

or navigating conflict helps people to feel safe with you, to know what to expect and to feel comfortable sharing their thoughts, feelings and emotions. You might notice there is overlap here between creating safe love with yourself and that's no coincidence. We will delve into this more in the next chapter, which is dedicated to emotions. We are just planting the seed here but this is a big one for creating a sense of emotional safety because when people don't fear how you will respond, they can be themselves, honest and open. If they're afraid of you becoming dysregulated, withdrawing or shutting down then they feel they need to censor themselves.

3. **Welcoming feedback.** This is very much associated with growth, learning and improvement. When we welcome feedback we are creating a space where we actually want to know how our words, behaviours and actions affect our partner/s and are open to improving and adjusting. We actively seek out opportunities to create deeper connections by asking about their needs and experiences.

4. **Accepting their emotions, and your own.** Emotions can be incredibly uncomfortable at times, especially when they are directed at you. Often, instead of sitting with emotions and validating them, we try to push them away, challenge them or become defensive. By accepting your emotions, you allow yourself to feel them and let them go. By accepting your partner/s' emotions, even when uncomfortable, you are supporting them to do the same. On that note, accepting emotions *does not* mean accepting all behaviours. There's a difference. We do not need to accept all behaviours, nor should we.

5. **Maintaining respectful communications.** This means learning to communicate respectfully, even when in conflict, and being

mindful of how your past wounds, patterns and parts may try to take over. It's about being willing to explore the patterns and responses that get you nowhere, and being willing to do things differently so conflict can actually become an opportunity for growth and knowing one another more deeply.

6. **Considering their needs**. Consideration is one of the highest forms of love in my opinion. Being considerate means thinking about how our choices, words and actions affect others. It is about valuing them, taking their wants and needs into account and thinking about the 'we' not just the 'me'.

Of course, this goes both ways. If we are doing the work to be a safe partner, we also need to be in a connection where the goal is mutual and the work isn't one-sided. Doing this work isn't easy. It takes a lot of courage to look at yourself, at your patterns and the areas you need to improve. It's easier to avoid looking at our past and really grappling with the ways our childhood and past relationships affect the ways we show up and respond in the present but that's what it takes to be a safe partner.

We have to be willing to do the work and take a long hard look at ourselves. We need to be open to accepting feedback, to making changes and navigating issues together as a team. If you're someone who is willing to engage in this process, who is committed to growth and wants to improve your relationship with both yourself and with others – which I am guessing you are if you are reading this book – then it's important you know that you deserve to have someone who values this work as well. They don't have to be fully healed, they don't have to be as far along in the journey as you are, but they do need to value it.

If you value growth, healing and want to consciously co-create a great relationship then that also needs to be a priority to the person or people you choose to be in a relationship with because you can't do it alone. You can work on your part, sure, but a relationship is an entity in itself and it is created by the people in it. You cannot create a safe relationship alone. This is why it's important to be able to identify what you need from a partner to create safe love in return.

What we need in order to feel safe and secure in a relationship

- **Emotional availability.** To be 'emotionally available' means your partner/s are willing to share their emotions, to grow, to connect and to create closeness with you. It means they can let you in enough to share emotional intimacy. When you are emotionally available but your partner/s or the person or people you're dating are not, it can create a lot of anxiety. It can feel like you're reaching out and trying to connect, but you just can't quite get close to them. Maybe you have moments of closeness when they let their walls down, but then they quickly close themselves off again and it leaves you feeling confused. We all have different levels of emotional availability, depending on attachment, past experiences and capacity, but trying to build safe love with someone who is not available can be difficult and painful.

  I don't say this to give shade to those struggling to be emotionally available. I was that person in my twenties. I was totally avoidant and emotionally unavailable but at the time, I had no idea. I wanted to be ready, I thought I was open. I wanted love but didn't realise I wasn't available to it. I was so driven to protect myself I couldn't let anyone close. I would start out open for the first month or so then as soon as it began to get real and they became invested, I pulled away. I didn't know the effect it had on the people I dated. I honestly thought it was them. I thought they became 'full on' or 'intense' all of a sudden. I didn't realise they were reacting to my withdrawal and this made them feel insecure.

As I have worked on myself over the years, learned to let my walls down and become more available, I realised it wasn't them at all . . . it was me! I have since been on the other side of it. On the side of being the one who is available and reaching for connection only to be left in confusion and pain when the person I was dating disconnected. It hurts because we all yearn for connection, to belong and to feel close. The reality is safe love requires a level of emotional availability and sometimes, they're just not there yet.

- **Emotional responsiveness.** To be emotionally responsive is to be able to observe, comprehend and respond to your emotions (most of the time). It is a process of being attuned to your emotional state, noticing when something is off and being curious about it. It's about being empathetic, considering your wants and needs and how things affect you and responding in a supportive way. I say most of the time because let's be honest we all have our days where we totally stuff it up, but we need a level of emotional responsiveness in order to feel loved, considered and like the way we feel is important.
- **Care.** We all want to feel cared for and important to the partner/s we choose. We want to feel care through their words, behaviours and actions. We want to feel like they genuinely want us to do well, that they're thinking about our wellbeing and are supporting us. This care might be displayed through affection, spending time together, or them being thoughtful, or considering our needs. What makes you feel loved and cared for will vary according to who you are and how you like to be loved, but regardless, feeling cared for is something we all need.

- **Willingness.** As I have said many times already and will continue to say throughout this book, it is not about perfection, it's about a *willingness* to do the work, get curious about our stuff and do what it takes to make change. Past experiences often leave us with wounds, unhelpful patterns of behaviour and unrealistic beliefs and expectations. We need to be willing to honestly look at how past relationships influence the way we show up. If we don't, we can end up holding current partner/s accountable for past partner/s' bad behaviours. We can obsess over what a partner is doing and forget to look at ourselves. When it comes to problems and issues in relationships, if you have one person willing to do the work, and another who refuses, you'll get stuck. You can't grow, you can't improve. We'll explore how to actually show up to this process in later chapters but for now, the willingness to look at our own behaviour and how it affects our partner/s is vital. It is something we all need for safe love.

- **Freedom.** Freedom is the ability to maintain your autonomy and individuality while in a relationship. It is the ability to feel free to pursue the things that are important to you, to grow and to show up as you are. It is knowing that you can take personal space without it being a threat to the relationship and feeling like there is respect for your personal boundaries. It is having the liberty to maintain connections outside the relationship and build a full and individual life while also having a connected relationship. When it comes to relationship education there is often a huge focus on togetherness and connection and while that is important, so is individual freedom. A big part of safe love is feeling free to be you, while also maintaining the relationship. Safe love does not require you to sacrifice fundamental parts of yourself, rather, it is a space that allows you to be more fully you.

We need these elements to create safe love. We need them because they create a feeling of safety. You can actually feel the difference between love that feels safe and love that doesn't. When love feels unsafe, you might find you struggle to open up, or feel on edge or anxious. You might have difficulty being vulnerable or sharing your thoughts and feelings with your partner. You might struggle to trust them or not feel like you can rely on them. This experience might be conscious in the form of thoughts you have about your relationship, or somewhat unconscious and be a felt sense in your body.

Safe love does not require you to sacrifice fundamental parts of yourself, rather, it is a space that allows you to be more fully you.

Signs there is a lack of emotional safety

- **Feeling on edge.** You may often feel anxious or on edge and worry about how your partner/s will respond to your needs, feelings, boundaries or choices.
- **Feeling like expressing yourself openly will result in negative consequences.** You might fear expressing yourself because doing so has resulted in negative consequences in the past or in them disconnecting which felt like a punishment.
- **You don't trust them.** You might find it difficult to believe what they say, or find yourself trying to catch them in a lie.
- **You are losing yourself.** You don't feel like you can be yourself so you start making yourself small to avoid conflict, disagreements or criticism.
- **A feeling of unease or tension.** There is an undercurrent of something not feeling right and maybe you notice it in your body.

- **You hide how you feel, what you think or need.** You have given up communicating how you feel, what you need or your perspective because you learned that doing so did not lead to anything good.

The difficulty here can be differentiating between the things that our hyperactive protective parts tell us are unsafe and the things that *are* fundamentally unsafe. There is a difference between what is hard but navigable and what is unsafe and/or abusive.

Things that are hard but you can learn to navigate include:

- It can be hard and take time to navigate the balance between different needs around closeness and separateness, but it is possible.
- Learning to really hear one another and respond to each other's needs can be a bit of a process, but it is achievable.
- It can take work to better manage conflict and communication in a way that promotes growth and respect, but it can be done.
- It can take time to learn how to better manage your emotions so your parts don't hijack you and you can respond rather than react, but it is doable.
- It takes a lot of vulnerability to be accountable for our dys-regulation in times of stress and overwhelm and to make real change for the betterment of ourselves and the relationship, but it is attainable.
- It can take a real willingness to look at our stuff and take ownership for what it brings to the relationship and to learn to better manage it, but it is achievable.

These are things that are hard, sure, but they can be achieved when the willingness, accountability and action are there. The things that make a relationship physically, emotionally, spiritually or intellectually unsafe are things like:

- **Manipulation.** Manipulation is when someone attempts (consciously or not) to influence you, control you or change your thoughts, feelings, behaviours or actions to benefit themselves. You might notice lies, passive-aggressive comments that make you question yourself, or guilt-tripping (making you feel bad about your decisions or choices to alter your behaviour). You might feel like they project their own uncomfortable thoughts, emotions, behaviours, or actions onto you. They might play the victim to make you feel guilty or sorry for them, or use silent treatment to shut down anything they don't want to talk about. Often there will be emotional outbursts so there is no space for you and your emotions and you have to put all your feelings aside to soothe them.
- **Gaslighting.** The dictionary defines gaslighting as 'psychological manipulation of a person usually over an extended period of time that causes the victim to question the validity of their own thoughts, perception of reality, or memories and typically leads to confusion, loss of confidence and self-esteem, uncertainty of one's emotional or mental stability, and a dependency on the perpetrator'.[5] Gaslighting essentially makes you doubt your ideas, feelings and experiences.
- **Heightened emotional dysregulation.** This might be in the form of adult tantrums which result in big, unsafe displays of emotions and behaviours that leave you feeling like you're walking on eggshells and concerned for your emotional or physical safety.
- **Possessiveness.** Possessiveness is the desire to dominate, control and assert ownership over another person. Possessiveness, like control, aims to isolate you and is often a precursor

to abuse. Someone who is possessive might want to constantly text, know where you are all the time, do everything together and say negative things about your friends in an attempt to stop you from spending time with them.

• **Any behaviour that attempts to control you, limit your independence or freedom.** Coercive control, more specifically, is a pattern of behaviours aimed at gaining power and control. It can involve manipulation, gaslighting, possessiveness, threats, humiliation and put downs, isolation from your support system, intimidation, name-calling and severe criticism. Coercive control is very serious and has been linked with intimate partner homicide.[6] I am not saying this to scare you. I am saying this because many of us feel guilt and shame about ending relationships and leaving people we love even if they are hurting us. But we cannot, I repeat we *cannot* build healthy relationships with people who are coercively controlling.

• **Any type of physical violence** whether that be pushing, shoving, throwing things or behaving in ways that make you fearful.

This is not an exhaustive list but rather a few examples of things that make relationships unsafe. If you are reading this and think that you may be in a relationship where unsafe behaviours are occurring, please go to the resources page at the end of the book and/or contact your local domestic violence support service. If you want to learn more about coercive control, *See What You Made Me Do* by Jess Hill is a brilliant yet confronting book that examines the crisis of domestic abuse in Australia.

—

Safety is the foundation. It's the foundation for being able to navigate conflict. It's the foundation for productive communication.

It's the foundation for great sex and intimacy and for building and sustaining healthy, loving relationships. Safety is where it all begins. Safety within yourself and safety in connection with your partner/s. That is why an entire chapter has been dedicated to it. The challenge is we all have at least a few things we do that may be unproductive. That's why the rest of this book is dedicated to helping you navigate those challenges, working through those issues, improving your communication and emotional regulation, and repairing the bond after ruptures inevitably arise. It contains everything you need to co-create the relationship you really want but maybe never thought possible.

Summary

- 'Safe love' is love that feels secure, respectful, supportive, consistent and stable.

- Creating safe love is an active process. It is something that we do together and it takes time, commitment and care.

- It's not just about *finding* a safe partner, it's about *being* a safe partner because we need both of those elements to create a safe relationship.

- Building a better relationship with yourself involves validating your needs, deepening your self-awareness, building self-trust, improving your emotional regulation, accepting yourself, being kind to yourself, letting more joy in, learning about your wounds, holding yourself accountable and treating yourself with respect.

- Being an emotionally safe partner requires you to learn the skills and tools which enable you to show up in a way that is consistent, respectful and responsive. It involves building trust, improving your emotional regulation, welcoming feedback, accepting emotions, maintaining respectful communication and considering your partner/s' needs.

- Most of us will need emotional availability, emotional responsiveness, care, willingness and freedom to create and sustain safe love.

- Being a safe partner is a choice. It's about choosing to do the work and adjusting where necessary to help your partner/s feel safer with you. It's about creating a space where you can thrive individually – and together.

Activity

Let's explore how you can create safer love with yourself and others. Reflect upon the following:

1. Refer back to the ten elements of building a better relationship with yourself.
   a. Which of these do you feel you do well?
   b. Which of these would you like to improve?
   c. What small commitment could you make to yourself to work on these areas in the next month? What might that look like in action?

2. Refer back to the six elements of being an emotionally safe partner.
   a. Which of these do you feel you do well?
   b. Which of these would you like to improve?
   c. What small commitment could you make to work on these areas in the next month? What might that look like in action?

4

Emotions

How your emotions affect
your relationship

All emotions are natural – whether you're feeling happy, sad, angry, disappointed, joyous, fearful or anything in between! They're also useful. Why? Because they are *information*. They are telling us what is happening in our internal world. It's not our emotions that cause issues in relationships, it's what we do with them and how we communicate them.

Emotions themselves are 'neutral'. There aren't any bad emotions although there are some that are more uncomfortable than others. Your upbringing and how emotions were responded to in your family of origin guides which emotions are more comfortable and which are seen to be acceptable.

You may never have noticed, but you have feelings about your emotions. These feelings are called 'meta emotions'.[1] These are determined by the way your emotions were responded to in childhood. In relationships this means you might struggle to sit with or respond to certain emotions expressed by your partner/s. When it comes to managing emotions, developing awareness is key.

Your emotional awareness and the way you regulate your emotions contribute massively to the state of your relationship. Our intimate relationships are often where we get most 'activated'. This occurs because these relationships are with the people closest to us. It doesn't help that many of us also choose partners who mirror our childhood dynamics.

Developing emotional awareness and improving your emotional regulation can drastically improve your relationships as well as your own internal experience. It requires you to become more attuned to your own emotions and the emotions of your partner/s, understanding their cause and effect, and learning how to manage them effectively. That is the purpose of this chapter.

Emotions

The way you feel affects the way you receive information and perceive events. The way you feel also determines how you interpret your partner/s' behaviour – more than you might realise. If you're tired, run down, frustrated or in a bad mood then you are more likely to interpret your partner/s' behaviour in a negative way. Your internal state significantly affects your relationship.

This is why stress is the cause of so many issues.

It's one of the big relationship destroyers and is closely connected to our level of relationship satisfaction.[2] Stress affects our communication making us more irritable and less able to navigate challenges effectively. It makes us prone to arguments and less able to see other perspectives. It makes it hard to be empathic. It can lead to a decline in intimacy and reduce feelings of closeness. It can make us feel emotionally distant and can result in you neglecting your partner.

But the reality is we live in a world where stress is unavoidable. Thankfully, it is manageable (most of the time)! Learning to manage stress is as important as learning to manage conflict because like conflict, you cannot totally avoid stress.

In order to manage it you first need to understand what's causing it. Then you need to work out what deactivates it. You can identify your stressors (that is, what stresses you out) by reflecting on the times you feel stressed. Is it connected with work and only while you're at the office? Is it connected with dealing with your difficult in-laws? Once you know what's causing it you can start to focus on ways to mitigate or manage it.

Dealing with stress requires you to take good care of yourself by getting enough sleep, staying hydrated, exercising, eating well and engaging in activities that promote relaxation and self-care. By doing all of this, you'll trigger the release of happy hormones which counter the effects of stress.

The happy hormones which help you mitigate stress are oxytocin, dopamine, serotonin and endorphins. Oxytocin is known as the love hormone and helps you feel calm, connected and content. You can trigger the release of oxytocin through physical touch which might be hugging someone, kissing or holding hands with your partner/s or even playing with an animal. Dopamine is known as the reward chemical. Dopamine makes us feel pleasure, motivation and satisfaction and is triggered by exercise, sex, eating something yummy or doing an activity you enjoy. Serotonin helps to stabilise your mood and helps you feel contentment, happiness and calm. It's triggered by getting enough sleep, eating well and getting some sunlight. Endorphins are known as natural painkillers and can make you feel energised and excited. Endorphins are released through exercise, sex, massage, eating and laughing.

Balancing and managing your stress through increasing the level of these happy hormones will help to alleviate the negative effects stress can have on relationships. The tricky thing is many of us don't have the emotional awareness or emotional intelligence to know when we need to take drastic action to mitigate stress.

The first step, therefore, is connecting with your body and emotions.

Feelings in your body

The terms 'feelings' and 'emotions' are often used interchangeably, however, when I say feelings, I am talking about the sensory experience, so what you feel in your body. I am talking about physical sensations like hunger, fatigue, anxiety, or arousal. We can experience physical sensations as a result of our emotional state.

Your body is always speaking to you through the way you feel. Paying attention to the sensations in your body is a valuable source of information. When we suppress emotions, it might present as digestive issues, sleep issues, pain, exhaustion or agitation. Similarly, we can often tell how safe and comfortable we feel with someone by how our bodies react in their presence. When there has been a build-up of negative interactions it can affect how you feel in your body. When something is off in the dating process, we feel it in our bodies. Noticing how you feel in your body is a helpful way to determine if someone you're dating is good for you.

So listen to your body. Make a habit of it. Set yourself a reminder to check in a few times a day and do a 'body scan' to notice how you're feeling.

Emotional intelligence

The ability to understand and manage our emotions as well as being able to observe and respond to emotions in others is called emotional intelligence. When you have high levels of emotional intelligence you are able to identify emotions in other people and respond with empathy. You are also better able to sit with your feelings and regulate your emotions. High emotional intelligence has a range of benefits including better relationships, improved performance in study and work, and better overall health.

Every day we can do small things which will increase our emotional intelligence. It starts with learning to pay attention to your emotions, sitting with any discomfort and noticing the links between your thoughts, feelings, emotions and actions. Many of us struggle to sit with uncomfortable emotions but the truth is they are always moving and shifting. They come like waves and never stay too long. No-one has ever died from feeling an emotion (that I know of) even though sometimes they can be incredibly overwhelming. Learning to sit with the discomfort of emotions you might perceive as negative is hard, but it can be learned.

Cognitive behavioural therapy (CBT) is one of the most effective and best-known approaches for helping you to understand the connection between your thoughts, feelings and emotions.[3] It goes like this:

- **Situation**. We experience a situation e.g. you get home and your partner hasn't done the dishes. You asked them to do the dishes before work and they said they would.
- **Thought**. Your thoughts about the situation create the narrative. You might think, 'I can't believe this! They didn't even listen to me. I bet they just expect me to do it again. Well, I refuse. I am not doing the dishes this time because it's their turn!'
- **Emotion**. This narrative and the thoughts you have about the situation then create the way you feel. In this case you will probably feel annoyed, frustrated and angry.

- **Behaviour.** The way you feel then drives your behaviour and actions. When you are feeling annoyed, frustrated and angry you can imagine the conversation you'll have when your partner gets home. It will likely become an issue, an argument and a source of conflict.

Now, this example shows one way of interpreting this particular event. The key to having a different outcome and changing the way you feel is to change the way you *think*. Say you get home and see the dishes in the sink. Instead of thinking your partner left them there on purpose, give them the benefit of the doubt. Maybe there's a reason the dishes are in the sink. Maybe an urgent call came through and they had to run out the door.

The key to having a different outcome and changing the way you feel is to change the way you *think*.

Imagine you're waiting for them to get home filled with anger and resentment and when they do, they tell you they got an urgent call because their mother was sick. How would you feel then? It's a big narrative change. Sure, it's possible they plain forgot, but the point is, the way you *think* about situations affects how you *feel* and then how you *behave*.

Increasing your emotional intelligence involves becoming more aware of your emotional experience. It involves tuning in and noticing what is happening in your mind and body in the moment. It requires presence which, in all honesty, is something most of us rarely practise because we are so focused on the past or future (or absorbed by a device).

To start increasing your emotional intelligence and awareness, try practising these steps.

1. **Pay attention to your emotions.** Regularly check in with yourself throughout the day. You might like to set a reminder on your phone twice a day to take sixty seconds and tune into your body. Ask yourself: how does my body feel? What thoughts am I thinking? How present am I?

2. **Sit with an emotion.** When you feel an emotion coming up just allow yourself to sit with it, follow it, and notice how long it stays around and how its strength shifts and changes. Notice when the emotion fades and if there is anything in particular that triggers its return.

3. **Notice the link between your thoughts and emotions.** Use the CBT process above to better understand the link between thoughts and emotions. How do your thoughts influence how you feel?

4. **Work on developing your emotional vocabulary.** Most people know very few feeling and emotion words. We might use the term 'sad' to describe being worried, disappointed, hopeless, lonely, hurt, powerless or overwhelmed. Being able to differentiate between emotions helps you to better understand and communicate what you are feeling.

By doing all of this, you will develop a better understanding of what is happening for you in the moment. This is an important precursor to improving emotional regulation.

Emotional regulation

Emotional regulation is the ability to understand and effectively respond to emotions and experiences. Helpful emotional regulation strategies include talking to friends, exercising, resting, journalling or taking a break from a conversation when you feel yourself becoming overwhelmed. Emotional *dysregulation* is the inability to effectively regulate your emotional responses and then reacting in ways that may be unhelpful. This might include becoming aggressive and projecting the issue back onto the other person, guilting or shaming them, or using alcohol or other drugs to numb your emotions.

People who experience mental health conditions such as bipolar disorder, borderline personality disorder (BPD), attention deficit and hyperactivity disorder (ADHD) and post-traumatic stress disorder (PTSD) may struggle more with emotional regulation but that doesn't mean improvements are impossible. Quite the opposite. While it might take more work, there are effective methods of improving emotional regulation and the effects of doing so on relationships are vast. Dialectical behaviour therapy (DBT) has been shown to contribute to positive improvements in emotional regulation and the strategies used are simple and actionable. One of my favourite DBT strategies is called 'STOP'.[4] When you feel yourself becoming emotionally dysregulated:

- Stop! Pause and stop what you are doing. Take a breath.
- Take a step back and do not react or do anything. You may feel overwhelmed by emotions that make you want to do something but fight that urge and just take a moment.
- Observe what is going on both internally and externally. What are you thinking and feeling? What sensations do you notice in your body and where?
- Proceed mindfully. Pay attention to how you are feeling, your thoughts and how they are guiding how you want to act, then make conscious decisions about how you want to move forward.

Implementing a practice like STOP, while difficult to do in the moment, can be a lifesaver for your relationship. Taking a pause and really considering how you are feeling before proceeding means you are *responding* rather than *reacting*. Responding takes time, consideration and presence. It involves noticing how you are feeling and thinking and then engaging in a conscious way.

Taking a pause and really considering how you are feeling before proceeding means you are *responding* rather than *reacting*.

Reacting, on the other hand, is instinctive, emotionally charged and usually driven by past experience. It is often immediate and unproductive. Reacting is when you are most likely to say things you don't mean, be unreasonable, unfair or just plain mean and then regret it later. We can't get our words back once they've come out of our mouths so being considered with our words is an important skill to learn. Using the STOP method, you can move from reacting into responding.

Emotional flooding

'Flooding' is another way of describing emotional dysregulation. It's when you become so overwhelmed with emotion in response to a situation, your thinking brain goes offline and you react from an emotionally driven state. You are unable to think clearly, understand others effectively or communicate productively. You go into your stress response – fight, flight, freeze or fawn – and might experience physical sensations such as a racing heart, sweaty palms and shallow breathing.

Your stress response is your go-to reaction when you perceive a threat – whether it's real or imagined. Someone who goes into fight mode will likely become angry or aggressive; someone who is more inclined to flight mode may totally remove themselves from the situation; someone who goes into freeze mode will likely shut down; and someone who goes into fawn mode may resort to people-pleasing.

These are all normal coping and self-preservation strategies and are nothing to be ashamed of. However, they are tendencies to be aware of as exhibiting any of these behaviours for long periods of time can become damaging.

Triggers and activators

Originally, a 'trigger' was considered an emotional response in the present moment that was influenced by past (usually traumatic) events, memories or feelings. When we're triggered, we become hijacked and overwhelmed which creates the feeling of being emotionally flooded. It's like you get a rush of feelings and hormones sending you into your stress response – fight, flight, freeze or fawn.

Triggers can be a result of a smell, hearing a certain word, phrase or tone; it might be something you see, or it might be being touched in a certain place. When it happens, it's as if you are transported back to a time when a threat was real and you felt the need to protect yourself. This happens even if right now you are perfectly safe. When we're triggered, it is very difficult to have productive conversations, to think clearly or navigate any kind of conflict because our thinking, rational brain essentially goes offline.

Now, the meaning of the word 'trigger' has changed due to popular culture, however I still prefer to differentiate and where there is no connection with past trauma, I like to use the term 'activated'. Becoming activated is when we have a strong emotional response to someone's behaviour (the way they do something), their actions or their words. We might experience a similar emotional or physiological response as when someone is triggered however it is not generally connected with trauma.

In relationships we all get activated from time to time. The goal is not to avoid becoming activated, but rather to notice when it happens and see it as an opportunity to more deeply understand yourself and learn how to better navigate the situation together. When something your partner says or does activates you, treat it as a chance to learn and explore. It often provides clues about unresolved issues, resentments or frustrations you may need to work on.

When you do find yourself activated, first of all you need to self-soothe. Once you are feeling grounded and have the capacity to reflect try asking yourself:

- What narrative or story do I have in my mind about the situation, event, behaviour or comment? What is the story I am telling myself?
- Do I have any memories or past experiences that are leading me to respond to the present moment in this way?
- Do I have a belief, dream or value which is guiding the way I feel?
- What emotions are coming up for me right now and driving the way I am responding?
- What do I need from myself or my partner right now?

Asking yourself these questions will help you to better understand what is driving your emotional reaction and why you've been activated. This allows you to work together and determine the best way forward.

Self-soothing

Self-soothing is the practice of engaging in activities which help you regulate your emotions. It is the process of soothing feelings of distress to help you return to a regulated emotional state. People self-soothe in many different ways. You might do it through exercise, journalling, meditating, breathing exercises, EFT tapping, listening to music, talking to a friend, challenging negative self-talk, stretching your body, having a bath, or doing grounding exercises. The key is working out what is best for you and then noting it down for when you need to access some strategies. The purpose of engaging in self-soothing is to activate the body's parasympathetic nervous system which helps to reduce feelings of stress and promotes calm.

Self-witnessing

Self-witnessing is the process of simply being present and noticing what is happening for you in the here and now. It's near impossible to do if you've just been triggered or activated but can be done once you have regulated and self-soothed.

To practise self-witnessing start by pausing and taking a long deep breath. Tune in and notice what is happening in your body. Are you feeling any tension? How is your heart rate? Pay attention to the sensations and take a moment to simply notice your breath and heart beat.

Once you're present and grounded, listen to the thoughts in your mind. What are you thinking? How do they influence the way you are feeling? Once you've noticed the narrative, acknowledge the thoughts and let them pass. Release them by accepting their presence and bringing your attention back to the here and now.

Strategies

This chapter wouldn't be complete without leaving you with some activities you can practise when you become emotionally flooded, activated or overwhelmed. Find the ones that work for you and practise them whenever you need. I recommend creating a personalised list you can refer back to. Here is a range of somatic tools to help you regulate.

- **Breathing.** Deep breathing is a very good way to regulate. Simply taking long deep breaths completely filling and emptying your lungs helps stimulate your parasympathetic nervous system. You could always follow a breathwork session on YouTube.
- **Grounding.** Putting your feet into the earth and spending time in nature.
- **Exercising.** Working up a sweat any way you choose – walking, running, yoga, Pilates, boxing, swimming or dancing. As long as you're moving it will work.
- **Cold exposure.** Try taking a cold shower or applying an ice pack to your neck.
- **Hugging.** Touch can be incredibly soothing. Being skin to skin with someone you love or hugging them can help you co-regulate and achieve a sense of calm.
- **Meditation.** Meditating has been shown time and time again to be extremely effective. If you're new to it, there are a wide variety of guided mediations on YouTube as well as many dedicated meditation apps available.
- **Heat.** Take a nice warm bath or lie down with a heat pack in the middle of your chest.
- **Play.** If you have a pet or a young child, playing with them can be a great distraction and help you to regulate.
- **Distraction.** Call someone or do something that takes all your attention and energy.
- **Stretching.** Lie down on the ground and stretch your body. Use slow and deliberate movements and focus all your attention on how it feels.

- **Napping.** This isn't for everyone but if you're someone who can nap when stressed (I totally can) then it can be a wonderful reset. Something about having a sleep works wonders for me.
- **Stimulating the vagus nerve.** The vagus nerve is the main parasympathetic nerve so stimulating it sends a message to your brain that you are safe and it's okay to calm down. While many of the strategies above stimulate the vagus nerve, there are also a few specific techniques you can try including singing, humming, chanting, gargling or laughing. The vagus nerve is connected to your throat and neck so the vibrations help to stimulate it.

Which of these suggestions sound like something you'd be willing to try? Next time you feel yourself becoming activated give them a go. Work your way through the list and see which is best for you. The goal is to help you return to a regulated state so that you don't react poorly towards your partner/s when you're hijacked by emotions.

Summary

- Emotions are a valuable source of information that tell us what is happening in our internal world.

- Stress can affect your communication, make you argue more, reduce your desire for intimacy and lead to you deprioritising your relationship.

- The 'happy hormones' which help you to manage stress are oxytocin, dopamine, serotonin and endorphins.

- The ability to understand and manage our emotions as well as being able to observe and respond to emotions in others is called emotional intelligence.

- Emotional regulation is the ability to understand and effectively respond to your emotions and experiences. Emotional dysregulation is the inability to effectively regulate your emotional responses.

- A trigger is an emotional response in the moment that is influenced by past (usually traumatic) events, memories or feelings.

- Becoming activated is when we have a strong emotional response to someone's behaviour, actions or words.

- Self-soothing is the practice of engaging in activities which help you regulate your emotions.

- Self-witnessing is the process of being present and noticing what is happening in the here and now and in your body.

Activity

Window of tolerance

The 'window of tolerance' concept was developed by the American psychiatrist Dr Daniel Siegel.[5] When we are within our 'window' – in other words our optimal emotional zone – we are able to function well. This means feeling good, relating well to others, communicating well and being able to emotionally regulate. This is the ideal state of 'arousal'.

Over time, due to our emotional experiences, environment and circumstances, we move in and out of our window. When we move into *hyper*-arousal we might feel anxious, stressed, restless, overwhelmed or agitated. When we move into *hypo*-arousal we might feel numb, checked out, exhausted, depressed or withdrawn. The size of people's window of tolerance will vary according to their childhood experiences, circumstances and experience of past trauma. The goal is to give you a practice that will enable you to start widening your window as that will help to improve your emotional regulation and awareness.

Here's how to increase your window of tolerance:

- Set a reminder on your phone to check in twice a day. Take a moment to notice how you're feeling in your body and what state of arousal you are in according to the window of tolerance.
- If you are either hyper- or hypo-aroused ask yourself what you need to help you move back into your window of tolerance.
- Practise breathing deeply and connecting with yourself and your body in the present moment.

- Managing stress is an effective way to increase your ability to stay in your window.
- Practise the self-soothing strategies mentioned earlier in the chapter when you find yourself moving into a hyper- or hypo-aroused state.

PART TWO

ALL ABOUT US

5

Co-creation

Great relationships aren't found, they are created

You don't just find a great relationship, you build it from the ground up. Great relationships are created by the people in them. When dating, you shouldn't be looking for a relationship per se, you should be looking for a partner. A partner who has the potential to co-create something amazing with you.

Great relationships are a result of the conscious choices we make to show up, be present and reflect on how our thoughts, behaviours and actions affect the dynamic. Sure, there are qualities a person may possess which give you a better chance of developing a strong bond, but in the end different people want different things, therefore figuring out what *you* want and how to consciously create it together is what counts.

Our culture has told us the ultimate goal, the thing that will make us happy, is finding the 'right' relationship. This is misleading. It's also a lot of pressure to put on someone. A relationship doesn't exist until you create it. How you come together, the way you respond to one another each and every day, and how you care for and nurture the relationship creates the dynamic you experience.

This means *you* have the power to create the relationship you want. You just need to find someone equally as committed to the process. You can overcome almost anything if you are *willing* to move out of self-righteousness and move towards collaboration and vulnerability. That's what true connection and commitment really need: a willingness for the 'we' to be as important as the 'me'.

Let me be very clear here. I am not saying 'we' to the detriment of 'me', I am saying 'we' is as important as 'me'. The problem is, our society has become so self-focused, so intent on pursuing and pushing our own individual needs that our ability to bend and adapt has become stunted. When we don't get our way we feel like we are sacrificing something. When that happens, we're liable to resent our partner/s for it.

Ultimately, we are not sacrificing for them, we are compromising for the good of the relationship. Co-creation is about creating the relationship environment you want to experience and that is a conscious process you move through together.

Co-creation

Creating a solid, satisfying relationship starts in the dating process. That's when you begin laying the groundwork. You need to get to know your potential partner. I mean, *really* get to know them. This means paying attention and seeing what they show you, listening and hearing what they tell you, and absorbing that information in order to paint a realistic picture of who they are . . . not who you want them to be. It's easy to get carried away projecting your hopes and dreams onto someone you are dating, creating a false version of them in your head, but this only leads to disappointment. The first step to conscious co-creation is accepting who your potential partner really is and getting to know their character . . . well!

Once you've got to know them and have decided this is someone you would like to create a relationship with, it's time for the second step: getting clear on the type of relationship and the type of relationship environment you want. The next step is 'walking your talk'. For example, do you want a relationship with open communication? Then you need to openly communicate. Do you want a relationship where conflict is managed respectfully and productively? Then you need to work at improving the way you manage conflict.

If you have a vision for your relationship, you need to actively show up and work towards creating it, not just expect your partner/s to do all the work or, even worse, expect it to *just happen with the right person*. This is another myth. Regardless of how well you are matched with someone, it won't always be easy. Co-creating a great relationship takes work and many people are unwilling or unable to put that work in.

If you have a vision for your relationship, you need to actively show up and work towards creating it, not just expect your partner/s to do all the work or, even worse, expect it to *just happen with the right person*.

It's bizarre really. Most people wouldn't just turn up on day one at a brand new job and expect to be proficient. You have to learn all the new systems and how the company runs because there will always be differences in this role compared to your last role. When it comes to relationships, however, we often have different expectations. You might expect it to be easy, or not require much work, flexibility or adjustment. With that attitude you won't be good at your new job . . . the job of being a great partner.

So what type of relationship do you want? That's the real question. Once you get clear on that you can start taking steps to create it. If you think of it like a position description for a job you're interested in, what would it sound like?

- **Position description**. Seeking full-time partner. Key responsibilities include the ability to communicate well, manage difficult conversations and emotionally regulate (most of the time).
- **Duties of the role**. Must be willing to navigate the ups and downs of life together and to take accountability when desired outcomes are not achieved.
- **Looking for someone who is emotionally available**, wants to connect, enjoys doing fun activities together and is looking for a long-term partnership.
- **Benefits**. Cuddles, emotional connection, sex and fun!

What is your position description for your partner/s or future partner/s? Is it realistic? Is it achievable? Most importantly, is it based on creating the relationship environment you want to experience? Finally, are *you* embodying that role?

Relationship environment

An environment is simply 'the circumstances, objects, or conditions by which one is surrounded'.[1] Therefore, your 'relationship environment' is the experience your relationship creates. It's how your relationship feels. Your relationship affects your mood, choices, emotions, stress, dreams, goals, likelihood of achieving said goals, life satisfaction and almost every other aspect imaginable. That's why creating an environment that is support-ive, safe, encouraging and positive is more important that most people realise.

The way you treat your relationship and your partner/s influ-ences the dynamic you create. Do you make your relationship a priority? Do you actually put time aside to chat after work, or do you just sit on your phones together, side by side, scrolling through social media? Do you make time for sex and intimacy? Do you schedule quality time together? Do you save energy for your partner/s or expend it all at work?

When you've been together for a while it's easy to become com-placent. Sooner or later, they're no longer getting the best parts of you anymore, not like they did when you were dating. They get the leftovers. The way you show up to your relationship creates the environment. And the main ways you create it are:

- How you treat your partner/s.
- How you speak to your partner/s.
- How you think of your partner/s, in other words, the narrative you create about them in your mind.
- The choices you make that affect your partner/s.
- How much you include your partner/s in your life.

Of course, it goes both ways and how they treat you has the same effect. Your relationship environment is like a delicate ecosystem. It is built through the ways you engage with each other, how you treat one another, and the choices you make, each and every day.

Create the environment you want

You *can* create the environment you want. This is the beautiful thing about conscious co-creation. You can make an environment that works for you and your partner/s. It doesn't need to be like anyone else's relationship environment, it can be tailored to *your* wants and needs. But in order to do this you need to know how.

The way you create your relationship environment is through conscious co-creation, so first you need to figure out how you want your relationship to feel, then you need to take action and actually show up in a way that enables that environment to develop. This means being conscious of your words and how you communicate with your partner; it means being aware of your thoughts about them and the stories you tell yourself about who they are; it means thinking about the relationship as an entity in and of itself and considering how the choices you make affect it. It means prioritising the connection.

Step one is to get really clear on the environment you want to create. Step two is to live it and breathe it.

Showing up

To succeed in creating the environment you want you need to show up. You need to be *willing* to put in the effort and look at the areas you need to improve. You might start by exploring:

- How am I showing up in my relationship currently?
- How would I be showing up and what would I be doing if I were consciously creating the relationship I want?
- What's the gap? What do I need to start doing? Or stop doing?

Once you get clear on the steps you need to take and the things you need to change, you've got a plan of action. You might need to work on your listening skills, or communicate your wants and needs more assertively, or get better at apologising. You might need to start showing a bit more affection and appreciation, or work on being less critical. Whatever it is, you can start to consciously choose how you want to engage, not blindly and unconsciously responding based on the past.

Much of the time, the way we speak, what we say and how we act feels unconscious. This means we are not actively choosing how we are showing up. Many people will use this as a way to avoid taking responsibility when they do something that hurts their partner/s. Because they didn't mean to do it, they don't think they should be accountable. But the truth is, sometimes we are responding that way *by choice*.

At work, people tend to be much more aware of what they are saying and how they are behaving. They are mindful of their interactions. We are like this in the dating process too, but once we get comfortable most of us get lazy and complacent. *I've got them, they love me and they're committed so I don't need to try anymore, right?* Wrong! If you are capable of making conscious and mindful choices about how you engage with your colleagues, communicating in a balanced way and managing your emotions, then you also have the ability to do it within your relationship. This is a hard truth many people don't want to accept but these are transferable skills. We think it's normal to make this effort at work, but believe we shouldn't have to do it at home. Wrong! This is why you need to start practising 'presence'.

When you are present, you are here dealing with and responding to this moment, not some moment far away in the future or the past. As we saw in the last chapter, we can all become 'activated' which hijacks us and makes it difficult to be present, but there is also the day-to-day lack of presence which is what I am referring to here.

We live in an era where most of us are so focused on where we have to go, what we have to do, what happened yesterday or what will happen tomorrow that we are simply not present here in this moment dealing with the situation at hand. If we were, we would find it much easier to navigate challenges when they arise. Instead, we bring the past into it, we fight over subjective realities and try to determine who is right and who is wrong.

When you are fully present, you are focused on what is happening in the moment, how the relationship feels in the moment. You are responding to the issue in the here and now. This removes a lot of pressure as you are not trying to solve the world's problems all at once.

Practise presence

Practising presence is simple, however simple doesn't mean easy! Being present in your relationship will help you to connect more deeply with your partner and become a better listener. Being present is a key element of truly showing up. So, how do you do it?

You start by:

- Listening objectively when they are talking to you.
- Taking their perspective on board even if you don't agree with it. That means validating (this will be described in more detail later on).
- Reducing multitasking and giving them your full attention wherever possible.
- Noticing how you are feeling in the moment and communicating what is happening for you, especially during difficult conversations.
- Getting off autopilot and actively engaging in your relationship and connecting with your partner.

Presence is one of the most valuable gifts you can give someone. Think about it. How often do you *really* give your partner/s your full and undivided attention? How often do you put your phone away or turn off the TV and just connect? How often do you show up fully in the moment? For most of us, it's a pretty rare occasion. You may not be able to do this all the time, that's not a realistic goal, however, the more often you are able to be fully present, the more connected you will feel to your partner/s. Your relationship environment will become more positive because presence shows your partner/s they are a priority. It tells them 'you are important to me' and ultimately isn't that how we all want to feel? Important, prioritised and valued?

—

Creating a great relationship environment sounds like a bizarre and complicated process but it's really not. It's about making conscious choices moment by moment that will be good for your relationship. It's about making the effort to be present and showing your partner/s they are important to you. You do this when you are dating without thinking because you are trying to win them over. You are trying to show them what a relationship could be like with you.

Relationships require time, effort and attention. You really do get out what you put in.

But once you're together the effort often stops and that is where people mess up. We think because they're invested we don't need to try as hard but that devalues the relationship. I am sure you know what that feels like. Someone is great while dating but then a few months later their effort diminishes and you're left feeling let down and lied to because the picture they painted was not what you ended up with.

You need to paint a realistic picture, and then you need to keep maintaining the quality of that image if you are to sustain its beauty. Relationships require time, effort and attention. You really do get out what you put in. The question is, how much are you willing to put in?

Summary

- Great relationships are created by the people in them and built through intentionally showing up, putting in the effort and making conscious choices.

- The 'we' needs to be as important as the 'me', not to the detriment of 'me' but just as important.

- Your relationship environment is the space and experience you create when you come together. It is a delicate ecosystem built through the ways you engage with one another, how you treat one another and the choices you make.

- You can create the relationship environment you want by:
  - Showing up and putting in conscious effort.
  - Practising being fully present with your partner/s.
  - Getting off autopilot and fully engaging with your partner/s, helping them to feel valued, loved, important and prioritised.

Activity

Reflect on the following questions:

- What type of relationship do you want to experience?

- How would you describe this relationship in terms of behaviours? What would it look like? How might it feel?

- What type of relationship environment would these behaviours create? For example, trusting, safe, secure, peaceful, fun, sexually explorative, nurturing, encouraging.

- Are you showing up in a way that will help you create the environment you want? If not, what could you do differently?

6

Friendship

Building a foundation of friendship

I've always thought of a really good relationship as a deep friendship . . . with extras! Building a foundation of friendship is about knowing, accepting and embracing your partner/s for who they truly are. It's about loving them for their uniqueness, their quirkiness, their flaws and all. It's not about loving some parts of them and trying to change others.

It never ceases to amaze me how people date those they wouldn't ordinarily be friends with. Why would you do that? Chemistry, that's why! Chemistry clouds your judgement and leads you to make decisions you would not make if you were in your rational mind (I've been there!). Chemistry can make it feel like a forest fire when what you really want is a slow burn. Chemistry can lead you to choose people with whom you have nothing in common, who have different values and whose life-styles clash with yours. While that doesn't necessarily mean you can't make it work, it does mean there will need to be more acceptance of those differences and a willingness to learn to navigate them over the long term.

Choosing to surround yourself with good people is probably the most important decision you can make in life. This is because your friends and partner/s significantly and directly affect your happiness and wellbeing. They affect whether or not you work towards and achieve your goals. And they affect how you spend your time. So it's important to choose wisely.

Choosing to surround yourself with good people is probably the most important decision you can make in life.

In long-term relationships there are going to be ups and downs. There will be times where you feel connected intimately. At other times you will feel disconnected. What holds you together through the periods of disconnection is the friendship. So, first things first, don't date people you wouldn't keep as a friend unless it's casual and more about sex (which is fine if that's what you're looking for and everyone is on the same page).

Let's now talk about how to build and deepen the friendship. We'll explore how to create an unshakeable foundation for your relationship whether it's rebuilding and strengthening something already established, or using tools to build it with someone new. Whatever your circumstances, this chapter will teach you how to create strong foundations so that love, intimacy and security can thrive.

Who is your partner?

When we start dating, we are so curious about who this new person is, what they like and what they dislike. We spend hours and hours getting to know them. This helps us to feel close, intimate and connected, and gives us valuable information about exactly whom we are investing in.

As time goes on, however, and we become more committed and secure in the relationship, our conversations change. They move from being about connection, to being focused on life admin. They change from the central purpose of getting to know one another and connecting, to talking about who will do what and when. This is unavoidable because when we merge our lives we need to talk about life stuff, but we don't have to compromise the connection in the process.

It's easy to become complacent. We think we have figured them out which leads us to stop being curious. We stop exploring who they are, what they care about and what their dreams are because we think we know, so we store all that information, lock it up, decide that's who they are and assume they will never change. These ideas become agreements, often unspoken, about who this person is and it can become very limiting.

I don't know about you, but I have changed a lot just in the last five years, let alone the last ten. If I am expected to be the same person over this whole period of time and not change, grow and develop then I am really going to let some people down, and that's what happens.

We assume we know our partner/s so we stop being curious. We assume we know them so we don't ask what they are thinking and feeling. We assume we know them so we stop having connecting conversations and place them in this bucket that says, 'This is you, you're all figured out' and if they try and get out of that bucket all hell can break loose.

The thing is, people change, people grow, people evolve and if we're not open to that we are limiting ourselves, we are limiting our partner/s and we are limiting our relationships. We need to stay curious if we want to build and sustain a strong relationship.

A really good friendship is based on trust. We need trust in any friendship as it lays the foundations that enable us to feel secure. Trust helps us to know we can rely on them, can tell them things and be assured they won't be repeated to anyone else or used against us later on.

We need to stay curious if we want to build and sustain a strong relationship.

We also need acceptance if we are to feel comfortable being our full selves. I am lucky enough to have a group of friends I have known since high school. Since those days, as you can imagine, a lot has changed. Some got married, some had children, some focused on their careers and some travelled. But even through all of these changes, even through me coming out and being the only queer person in this group, we still accept each other. Those who remain close do so because they value the friendship, and they show it in their actions. We accept and support one another through the changes in lifestyle, location, career, relationships and sexuality, and continue to come back together and learn.

We are all allowed to grow and change. My friendships have evolved as we have grown. Some people have grown away from the group, and others have grown together making it stronger than ever before. I can't imagine anything could stop us from being friends after all this time and I hope I never have to face that reality.

Of course, we are more likely to support our friends when they're going through changes, embracing growth and exploring who they are and what they want because it usually doesn't threaten us. It doesn't threaten the life we want, the agreements we've made or the vision of the future we have for ourselves.

With partner/s, however, it *can* be threatening. When it comes to an intimate relationship it isn't just about them, it's about us. Sometimes it's easy to lose sight of the 'we' and become focused on the 'me'. We can become consumed with how their decisions affect us and this focus on self clouds our ability to be a really good friend to our partner/s. Creating solid foundations relies on us stepping out of being so self-focused and instead concentrating on the 'us'.

People change over time, and sometimes, that can be seen as a threat. It can feel like a threat to the relationship and to the bond and so we avoid addressing it. Really, change represents an opportunity to get to know each other more deeply. It represents an opportunity to take our partner/s out of the 'I know everything about you' bucket and start all over again. It represents the chance to create deeper, more meaningful connections. It represents an opportunity to reconnect and ask:

- In what ways do you feel like you've changed?
- Have your priorities changed since we first got together?
- Have the things you enjoy and do for fun changed?
- Do you feel like you've changed as a person e.g. your beliefs, values, interests?
- Do you feel like I am accepting of these changes?
- Have any of these changes affected our bond and connection in your eyes?
- Is there any way I could better support you?

We ask these questions to embrace the changes, to embrace the growth and face the fears that accompany them. We fear it because change challenges certainty. We want certainty because it gives us a perceived sense of control but we are never really in control. It's an illusion. An illusion we will fight tooth and nail to maintain and that does more harm than good. If we want to thrive, we need to embrace the uncertainty and discomfort that comes with change, growth and evolution.

If we want to thrive, we need to embrace the uncertainty and discomfort that comes with change, growth and evolution.

Build or deepen the friendship

Okay, so we know that friendship is important but how do you actually build a solid friendship with a potential partner or deepen the bond in an already established relationship? The answer is by practising dedication, respect, enjoyment, curiosity and acceptance – and creating a positive perspective. Let's break these down.

Dedication

We need to prioritise time with our partner/s. We need to actually make time to spend together and connect, to have fun and to play. We need to laugh. We need to be dedicated to making the relationship not just work, but thrive.

Often, we get bogged down with day-to-day mundane tasks, we talk mostly about life admin and we forget to make time for conversations that make us feel close. We stop listening and start multitasking while our partner/s talk to us. When we do this, they feel unheard, unseen and unimportant. This type of conversation drives disconnection rather than a feeling of closeness.

Yes, we need to have the task-based conversations to keep the day-to-day stuff going, but we must make time for the friendship too. Maintaining a close friendship requires time and effort. You need to make time to spend together. You need to prioritise each other. Don't get complacent. When you get complacent and forget to prioritise your relationship it suffers. You'll feel disconnected and over time like you're leading separate lives.

We're all busy and it can be difficult to find the time and energy to do all the things we want, however, if something is important to you, you *can* find the time. It might mean being a bit more organised, moving things around or even missing out on something else, but if it's important to you, you'll do it. Great relationships require a level of commitment, energy and dedicated time. That old saying 'you get out what you put in' is as true for relationships as it is for anything else.

Respect

One of the areas where I see the most trouble is when partners do not respect one another. This can happen when negative interactions build up over time. Respect is absolutely fundamental if we are to have a good friendship. Respect helps us to communicate kindly, to value their opinion, to listen to them, and to build trust and security. It fosters equality, mutual growth and fairness. It facilitates connection both emotionally and physically as it allows you to feel safe and comfortable with your partner/s. When the respect starts to fade – for whatever reason – we've got real problems because that's when the criticism and contempt can creep in. Without respect we don't have safety and without safety we cannot have a healthy friendship.

Enjoyment

Have you ever had one of those friendships where spending time together felt like a chore? Maybe they were a family friend or a colleague and you just didn't vibe. Maybe you even resented the fact that you had to hang out with them; maybe you found them a little annoying if you were to be totally honest. That's where some people end up with their partner/s when they've become really disconnected and filled with resentment. It sucks!

No-one wants to get to a point where they just don't enjoy one another's company anymore. Being stuck in that space is just plain miserable. Enjoyment of one another and the time you spend together is critically important for the friendship *and* for the health of the relationship. Enjoyment means appreciating your time together, having fun, and taking pleasure in connecting. It may not be your experience every moment of the day, but there needs to be a fair bit of enjoyment to balance out all the mundane stuff.

Curiosity

Stay curious about who your partner is. This means asking questions, actively listening when they are telling you stories and sharing information about their life, and being open to them changing. It means allowing them to be who they are in the here and now without becoming too attached to that version of them. It means allowing them to grow into the best version of who they are and doing your best not to be threatened by this. It means choosing them and the relationship each and every day.

Curiosity is especially important when it comes to keeping the fire lit. Imagine you find a sexual position that you both really enjoy. You know it works so you always have sex the same way. Chances are over time it's going to get boring. It's going to feel like a chore, there will be no excitement and eventually you'll probably just stop having sex altogether. It's the same with emotional connection. If you don't stay curious, ask questions and explore, then you can end up in a rut.

Acceptance

That feeling of being seen, understood and accepted is the holy grail. Isn't that what we all want? To feel loved and accepted for who we are? It gives you the freedom to grow, to explore and to thrive. It makes you feel like you belong. At a very basic level, this is what we all needed from our parents or caregivers. Unfortunately, many of us never received it, therefore, to find it in our adult relationships is incredibly healing.

This doesn't mean you have to accept harmful behaviours or traits by any means and it also should not be used as an excuse. People using the phrase 'that's just who I am' to explain away hurtful actions is a cop-out at best and manipulative at worst. Acceptance is about seeing and accepting your partner for who they are, not who you want them to be. It's about seeing their flaws and loving them all the same. It's about allowing yourself to be vulnerable enough for them to see the *real* you. It's about knowing there is no such thing as perfection.

Positive perspective

'Positive perspective', a term used in Gottman Method Therapy, was developed by Drs John and Julie Gottman. It essentially refers to being in a space where you see and experience your partner/s in a positive light.[1]

You can influence the way you feel about your partner/s and your relationship through your thoughts. This involves actively becoming aware of your thoughts about your partner/s and about your relationship. By doing this, you are able to choose which thoughts you engage with and also notice how they influence the way you feel.

Our thoughts and beliefs affect how we interpret situations and behaviours. This means, for example, that if you believe your partner is a selfish arsehole, guess what? Your brain is going to home in on any and all information it can find to confirm that belief. This is why we need to be aware of our thoughts and actively choose to focus on the things we love and appreciate about our partner/s.

Practising being aware of your thoughts won't only improve your relationship, it will improve your life! Your thoughts are incredibly powerful but many are unconscious and repetitive. When they are left unchecked they can drive disconnection, resentment and dissatisfaction; therefore you need to consciously create a positive perspective. In the context of your relationship, this involves reminding yourself regularly of all the things you love and appreciate about your partner/s. It requires you to express gratitude to them for the ways they help and support you. It means noticing the things that are going well and paying attention to what's working. By doing this regularly, you balance any negative experiences with all the positive ones you are actively working to identify.

Practising being aware of your thoughts won't only improve your relationship, it will improve your life!

Having a solid basis of friendship is fundamental because it's what will help you sustain the connection when times get tough. And they will! We need a foundation that allows us to show up for one another, to demonstrate care, consideration and kindness even when we haven't had sex in a while, or are stressed, or haven't had much sleep, or are feeling irritable. Most importantly, we need to *like* our partner/s' character. We need to like them as a person first and foremost. We need to respect them, appreciate them, enjoy spending time with them and we need to stay curious about who they are. If we can do all of this, we'll create deep foundations and long-lasting relationships.

Summary

- A solid foundation of friendship is at the heart of any great relationship. It's about knowing, accepting and embracing your partner/s for who they are. It's about loving them for their uniqueness, their quirkiness, their flaws and all.

- A solid friendship requires trust, acceptance, encouragement and the willingness to stop being so self-focused and instead concentrating on the 'us'.

- We need to stay curious and give our partner/s the freedom to grow and change. If we don't, we are limiting them, the relationship and ourselves.

- Build or deepen the friendship with your partner/s through dedication, respect, enjoyment, curiosity, acceptance and creating a positive perspective.

Activity

How well do you know your partner/s?

Who are they? What do they like? What makes them tick? Depending on how long you've been together you may know the answers to these questions, or you may simply *think* you know and be totally off base. Just because we knew them inside and out five years ago doesn't mean we know them that well now if we have not stayed curious.

Asking questions helps you feel closer, more intimate and builds the friendship. It helps you to know one another on a deeper level. Take a moment to consider the questions below. If you're in a relationship I encourage you to sit down with your partner/s and put these questions to them. See if any of their answers surprise you. It's an opportunity to learn more about them. If you're dating or unattached at present, you can pose these questions throughout the dating process.

Do you know:

- How they like to give and receive love?
- Their predominant attachment style and how that shows up for them in their behaviour?
- Their major life stressors at the moment?
- What helps them self-soothe, regulate their nervous system and feel better when they're activated?
- What makes them feel most loved?
- How their past, upbringing or previous relationships influence how they show up with you?
- How much alone time they need? How they communicate that need with you?
- How much together time they like?
- What their life goals and dreams are?
- What they love and appreciate most about you and the bond you have?

7

Me to We

It's not about me or you, it's about us

In the words of the American therapist and writer Harville Hendrix (channelling John F Kennedy), 'Ask not what you need from your partner, but rather, ask what does your partner need from you'.[1]

Have you ever noticed how 'me' focused Western society is? We seem obsessed with the experience of the individual over the experience of the collective. This creates a challenging dynamic in relationships as being 'me' focused all the time can make it very hard to collaborate and compromise. But both skills are essential if we want to live harmoniously with someone else.

In my work with folks in relationships, my client is not the individuals sitting in the room, it's the relationship. I think about the relationship as an entity. It's not just about me or you anymore, it's about us. Considering it in this way, we need to ask ourselves, 'What is best for the relationship?'. When you frame it like this, you are better able to compromise, collaborate and see your partner/s' needs as equally important as your own. When you are able to shift from being solely self-focused to being relationship-focused, you can find real balance and equality. You'll also create robust foundations. In a world that has taught us to be self-absorbed, we need to redirect our attention.

Because, in the end, it's *not* all about you. That might sound harsh but it's true and probably very different from a lot of the content you see on social media. We have become selfish as a society and the more selfish we are, the more disconnected we become and ultimately the less happiness we experience. So we need to shift the focus. We need to prioritise connection. We need to stop being so concerned with the 'me' and start redirecting our attention towards the 'we'.

We need to stop being so concerned with the 'me' and start redirecting our attention towards the 'we'.

Let me be very clear. I am not saying to focus on the 'we' to your own detriment. Creating a thriving relationship should *not* result in you losing yourself or sacrificing your own needs to the point of harm. It's not about losing your independence. In order for your relationship to flourish and be effective, it must be mutual. If you're the only one focusing on the 'we' then it ends up being unbalanced and one-sided. And that doesn't work.

Redirecting our attention towards the 'we' may feel like a threat to anyone who fiercely holds onto their independence (often those with avoidant tendencies . . . Hello you. I really resonate). But independence is *not* the goal in a relationship. If you want complete independence, then you're better off staying single and doing your own thing! If you want real connection, then *interdependence* is the goal. Interdependence describes a situation when you can rely on one another, you can get close but you still maintain your sense of self. It's when you have yourself, you have the relationship and your partner/s also have themselves. You don't have to give up who you are for the relationship. You can maintain a solid sense of self while also valuing and nurturing the relationship.

Interdependence is the goal if you want to create a relationship where you can thrive individually *and* together. The alternatives to interdependence are 'enmeshment', which is when we lose our sense of self and become consumed by the relationship; or 'detachment', where we are overly independent and unable to really let others in.

I am going to guess neither of these options is what you are hoping to achieve if you are reading this book! Let's explore the differences between these three styles of relating.

Enmeshed

In enmeshed relationships there tends to be too much closeness which results in you feeling like you're at risk of losing yourself. You might be overly affected by your partner/s' thoughts, beliefs, moods or emotions and have difficulty separating what they want and how they feel from what you want and feel. You may be overly reliant on one another and feel threatened by them having other important friendships and relationships. This might lead to a fear of abandonment. Imagine an ivy plant growing over the top of other plants. While it can be beautiful it can also be suffocating. The ivy can stop the other plants getting the light and nutrients they need to thrive.

The consequence of enmeshed relationships is there is usually very little space for individual wants, needs, goals or dreams. Personal boundaries are typically non-existent and while those involved may appear very close on the surface, there will likely be a lot of self-sacrificing and self-abandonment happening in order to maintain a sense of harmony.

Detached

At the other end of the spectrum, detached relationships lack emotional closeness and intimacy due to the avoidance of deep connection. The desire to protect the self from being overtaken is so strong it doesn't allow for any level of dependence. This prevents real emotional intimacy. If you're in a detached scenario, you may lead very separate lives and struggle to rely on your partner for emotional support. This in turn can lead to feeling lonely and disconnected.

Interdependent

In interdependent relationships (aka the goal) there will be a balance between independence and togetherness. You're able to maintain your sense of self while also being vulnerable, embracing emotional connection and support. You can depend on each other and also on yourselves individually. You'll have a balance between 'give and take' and mutual respect for one another's autonomy. This autonomy doesn't threaten the relationship or connection, in fact, it adds value. You can trust and rely on one another and as a result tend to feel like the relationship is emotionally fulfilling, secure, and encouraging of personal growth.

Interdependence is created through valuing both independence and togetherness. Through prioritising the relationship and also having a personal life. By continuing to pursue your own goals and dreams while also creating shared dreams. By learning about your partner, and about yourself, separate to the relationship. By communicating your wants and needs and also responding to the needs of your partner/s. Interdependence is created through the balance of you, me and us. It's about creating equality. A space where you are each responsible for yourself and can come together to create a shared life and experience.

Now, I am not sitting here telling you enmeshment and detachment are terrible and must be avoided at all costs. The truth is we might go through phases of all three styles, but it's where you find yourself most often that's important. You might feel a bit enmeshed in the honeymoon phase where you can't get enough of each other; later on you might go through a stressful period and feel a bit detached. When this happens, it's okay. It's unrealistic to expect you will never have periods in either of these styles. However, if you're stuck there for long periods of time, it can damage the connection.

When it comes to moving more towards a 'we' focus, the way you think about your partner and the relationship really matters. It creates the experience, therefore becoming fully aware of your thought patterns is essential.

There are four key concepts you'll want to familiarise yourself with in order to discover the effect of your thinking. They are your 'core narrative', your 'core wound', how and when you use a 'victim mentality', and the 'subjectivity' of your reality. By understanding these concepts you give yourself the power to choose. You can choose how you think and therefore how you feel. You can choose to focus on the 'we' and also understand a bit more about your individual 'me'.

Core narrative

In an intimate relationship, you create a narrative (or story) about your partner and this narrative guides how you interpret their words, actions and behaviours. The concept of a core narrative or a 'core negative image' comes from the American therapist Terry

Real in his book, *Fierce Intimacy*.[2] Terry talks about how we all have a core negative image of who our partner is and a heightened awareness of what we perceive their most negative traits to be. This image is not entirely a reflection of them and yet does have some basis of truth; it's just an exaggerated version of their flaws.

When they do something that aligns with the image we have of them, it's a big deal! We pay it a lot of attention and tend to get very self-righteous. However, when they do something that goes *against* this image, we often don't give it the same value.

It works like this: say you have an image of you partner as being a bit thoughtless and careless. They might often lose or misplace things. This annoys you as you are very thoughtful and careful. Every time they ask you where something is, it confirms this narrative of them being careless. You start to get frustrated because it seems like they lose something every day. Your brain starts to notice and emphasise all the times they lose something because it confirms the reality and belief you have created of them. However, it ignores all the times they find things easily, are thoughtful, careful or behave in ways that go against the narrative.

It's highly likely even though they lose their keys there are many other ways they are being thoughtful. You just don't notice. The key to managing the narrative of them being thoughtless and careless is first to become aware of it and second, to actually look for things that challenge the image you have created. This allows you to develop a more balanced view of your partner. And it makes for a happier home!

Core wound

Just as we all have a core narrative, we also have a 'core wound' that influences how we show up to and experience our relationships. Your core wound comes from your childhood and is often activated by your partner. Imago relationship therapy developed by Harville Hendrix says your core wound is usually what you wanted and/or needed as a child but didn't receive.[3] [4] It could be that you didn't receive the affection, or attention, or support, or respect, or feeling of being important that you always wanted. Maybe you didn't feel seen, or heard, protected or prioritised. This core wound then appears in the things that upset us, the things we need and the ways we desire to be nurtured.

Unconsciously we try to heal our core wound through our adult relationships. The only problem is, we often choose partners who find it very difficult to soothe us due to their own needs and their own wounding! Perhaps your wound is that you felt unimportant and like people didn't consider your needs or make you a priority. Maybe growing up you felt like your parents were so consumed with their own lives they didn't think about you and that your needs were unimportant. Independence was thrust upon you and you became extremely self-reliant. As an adult you then attract someone who is also either hyper-independent, which results in you feeling that same sense of being unimportant and not considered, or you attract someone overly anxious, which is a swing in the opposite direction but again, their anxiety is about them and not about you.

Either way, you attract someone whose focus on self will make it difficult for them to show up for you in a way that makes you feel important. This is why we need to talk about our core wounds. Once we know what they are, we can explain how they affect us and express what we need from others in order to feel safe, secure and validated.

Victim mentality

If you're always the victim then you are never taking responsibility. Having a victim mentality means you are always interpreting the world around you as if things are happening *to* you. When you have a victim mentality you are incredibly self-focused which makes it difficult to see the role you play in issues. It's almost impossible to have a healthy relationship with someone who is always in victim mode because in the majority of relationships it's not cut and dried (other than in cases of abuse).

When people are stuck in victim mode and refuse to see or acknowledge their part in issues it can actually become a form of emotional abuse. They will unknowingly gaslight their partners and distort reality because they are so attached to this narrative of them being the victim. They may completely misinterpret events in order to confirm their beliefs. This can be manipulative whether it's done consciously or not.

This commitment to being the victim can become abusive. There is such an ingrained belief in their victimhood that rather than taking accountability, they project their bad behaviours onto others and gaslight them into thinking it's them.

The victim mentality is a coping strategy that often comes from a childhood where they were, in fact, a victim. The sense of innocence and knowing they had no control over what happened to them helped them to manage difficult situations. However, they are now adults and they *do* have control. Sometimes we need to accept that it is our fault and seek support to change the narrative and develop more productive coping strategies. Being in victim mode doesn't help anyone and nor does it help a relationship. So, if you are reading this and realise that every issue in your life is always someone else's fault – your partner, parent, boss, co-worker, sibling – then this is your opportunity to work on your mindset.

—

Self-absorption and self-centredness can be a self-protection strategy. If we grew up in a household where our needs weren't met and we learned we had to fend for ourselves, we can become self-absorbed as a way of protecting ourselves and to make sure our needs are met. Sure, it's not the ideal way to approach a relationship, but when you think about it, it makes sense. If we were living in fear that we wouldn't be taken care of, be considered or have our needs met, it's natural we'd become hyper-focused on ourselves. We'd struggle to compromise and collaborate and might perceive a partner's attempt to meet in the middle as a threat to our needs not being met.

This was me in my teens and early twenties. I grew up with a father who wasn't emotionally available due to his own life experiences and circumstances. My mother died when I was two and I spent a lot of time alone. I became hyper-independent in order to manage my emotional experiences and this led to selfishness as a self-preservation strategy. I didn't realise I was doing it, but over time, as I became more secure in myself, I started to see it.

Many of my friends were more generous with their time, with their connections and with their resources, yet I was always focused on myself. I loved them, but I was living through the lens of self-preservation, not security. This was also evident in my relationships. I was focused on my experience, my needs and what they were doing to me . . . not what was happening for my partners.

When we are able to have compassion for the parts of us working so hard to keep us safe we are able to soften the ways they show up. While this strategy helped me get through childhood, as an adult it got in the way of me forming real, deep connections.

Your reality is subjective

When we fight, we are often fighting about whose inner world is more true or valid, or whose reality is more correct. We forget that two things can be true at once. You will never win a fight which hinges on making your partner believe the truth of your inner world or that your experience is more correct than theirs. It just won't happen. And yet, this is what so many of our fights are about: whose inner world and experience is more valid. Rather than accepting we all have different experiences, beliefs and inner worlds, we fight in order to make the other person feel the same as us or, even better, to admit we're right. But no matter how you swing it, you're *not* right. Not when it comes to another person's inner world.

The way everyone views and experiences the world is different. I like to think of it like this: imagine everyone in the world is wearing a pair of glasses. The lens in those glasses holds your values, beliefs, experiences, memories, wants, needs, hopes, desires, dreams and fears. Every time you open your eyes and take in the world around you, you do so through that lens. Because everyone's lens will be different, so too will be the way they see, interpret and experience the world. This is why you can have two people experience the same event and feel completely different about it.

When you're not conscious of your subjective reality, core wound, core narrative or victim mentality, it can wreak havoc on your relationship. Left unchecked it can lead to resentment, criticism, defensiveness, stonewalling and contempt. Drs John and Julie Gottman calls these four major predictors of relationship breakdown the 'four horsemen'.[5] If you want to avoid these, and I suggest you do because let's be honest they're awful, you need to focus on empathy, appreciation, fondness and a willingness to find a balance between give and take.

The importance of empathy in a relationship cannot be overstated. It is your miracle cure when it comes to navigating issues. Empathy is defined as 'the action of understanding, being aware of, being sensitive to, and vicariously experiencing the feelings,

118

thoughts, and experience of another'.[6] Empathy allows you to sit with your partner when they are experiencing challenges and give them support. It allows you to see and value their perspectives and feelings and it helps you to understand their experience. If you're good at practising empathy, your partner will likely feel seen, heard and understood. They will feel loved and valued.

Appreciation and fondness is the next step and adds another layer. Fondness is actually liking your partner which is pretty important if you ask me! You want to like them as a person first and foremost.

After that, you want to appreciate them. Appreciation helps you maintain a positive perspective because you are continuing to focus on the things you appreciate about them. When the appreciation starts to drop, the resentment starts to build and you want to avoid that as much as you can.

When you've got these three elements it's easy to balance give and take. This is because when you are able to empathise with your partner, when you appreciate them and when you are genuinely fond of them, you want them to be happy. And this makes it much easier to compromise. When you're feeling frustrated, resentful, bitter or defensive, the last thing you want to do is stop being self-focused and return to a balanced give-and-take situation. Hell no! Balancing give and take in a relationship means your needs are equally important and your partner/s' happiness is just as much of a priority to you as yours.

You might be thinking at this point, 'That's all great, Lucille, but how do I do this? How do I actually talk about this stuff with my partner?' I would respond by saying, 'That's a wonderful question' and it's *exactly* where we're heading in the next chapter. Now you know some of the things you need to talk about and explore, how do you actually have those conversations? Let's find out, shall we?

Summary

- Your relationship is not just about 'me' or 'you' anymore, it's about 'us'. This means we need to start asking ourselves, 'What's best for the relationship?'

- In 'enmeshed' relationships there's too much closeness which can result in you feeling like you lose yourself. 'Detached' relationships on the other hand lack emotional closeness and intimacy due to the avoidance of deep connection. In 'interdependent' relationships – the goal – there is a balance between independence and togetherness.

- You create a 'narrative' about your partner and this guides how you interpret their words, actions and behaviours.

- We each have a 'core wound' from our childhood and it's often activated by our partner.

- When we fight, we are often fighting about whose inner world is more true or valid, but you will never win that fight.

- Fostering empathy, appreciation and fondness will help you find a balance between give and take.

Activity

Reflect on the following questions about either a current partner or a past relationship:

- What narrative have you created about your partner/s? Who have you decided they are? How would you describe your core negative image of them?

- What core negative image do you think they have of you?

- Identify your core wound. What did you really want and need as a child that you did not receive? How could you give that to yourself now? How could your partner show up for you in a way that soothes that wound? How does this wound show up in your relationship and present challenges?

8

Communication

The art of communication in a relationship

The lifeblood of a thriving relationship is effective communication. Without it, no matter how much love there is, we can end up feeling frustrated, resentful, misunderstood and as though our needs aren't being met.

Our communication either helps us connect, or results in disconnection. We think that avoiding conflict will help us when really distance in a relationship is created through stepping back and staying silent. Disconnection starts in the words that are *unspoken*. Often, we avoid having hard conversations in order to protect our partner/s' feelings, or because we think we know how they'll react and want to avoid the 'drama'. We might even minimise issues and tell ourselves they're not so important when they really are. When we do this, we avoid short-term discomfort, but we sign up for reoccurring challenges in the longer term.

This is why learning to communicate effectively and 'fight clean' is so essential. In this chapter we'll explore how to have the hard conversations with one another and unpack what sometimes gets in the way. We'll cover practical and effective communication tools and strategies that you can implement right now. Then, in the next chapter, we'll learn about how to fight clean . . . because fighting and arguing are inevitable.

Why we hold things back

- **People-pleasing.** As a recovering people-pleaser, I know how the desire to please others stops you from speaking your truth, sharing what is bothering you or setting boundaries. People-pleasing is when the drive to please others results in self-sacrificing, self-abandonment, dismissing or minimising your own wants and needs out of fear of the repercussions or in order to avoid issues.
- **Conflict avoidance.** Many people believe that conflict is bad in relationships. They think it suggests something is wrong so they avoid it at all costs. The problem is, conflict can actually be a helpful tool. Conflict allows us to better understand one another and navigate differences. When we avoid it, we can end up feeling unseen, unheard, misunderstood and as though our needs are not important.
- **Fear.** The fear of creating issues and not wanting to be judged or seen as 'too much' or a 'bad' partner.
- **Protection.** Not wanting to hurt their feelings and believing that avoiding negative feelings is a better option than dealing with conflict.

The result of withholding

While the decision to withhold is often well-intentioned, it usually results in disconnection. This is because it erodes trust over time.

If you are keeping things to yourself that could affect your partner and they later find out, more than likely they're going to feel betrayed. This then can lead to breakdowns in communication as you are not openly communicating your needs and what is going on for you. Resentment inevitably builds because they might feel like they're being left out or not included. All of this can affect decision-making, balance and equality and create an atmosphere of distrust and inauthenticity where partners are not being open with one another or true to themselves.

This is why you need to communicate, not withhold. It doesn't mean you have to share *everything* – privacy is valid in many cases – but keeping something to yourself that could affect your partner is likely to lead to conflict later even if the act of withholding is an attempt to avoid it.

Interestingly, avoiding conflict and withholding often has a more detrimental effect on relationships than conflict itself. If you can learn to navigate disagreements effectively, then they can actually be *good* for your relationship. Being able to do this is heavily influenced by your communication skills. What skills do you need to be a good communicator and what are the blocks to communication? Let's start with the blocks.

Blocks to communication

- **Assumptions.** When we assume we fill in the blanks. We make up the information we don't know and act as if it's the truth. We often do this because not having all the information makes us feel out of control, so we seek control by assuming.
- **Talking over each other.** Sometimes people feel so overwhelmed by the need to say something and be heard they are unable to listen and are insistent on getting their point across.

- **Not actually listening**. Being distracted on your phone, watching TV or simply just not paying attention to what they are saying.
- **Judging and shaming**. Categorising their behaviour according to your opinion, values and beliefs and then putting them down when they don't fit your idea of how they should be.
- **Guilt-tripping**. Trying to make someone feel bad in order to get them to do what you want. Guilt-tripping is a form of manipulation, as it uses guilt to make someone change their behaviour, thoughts or actions in a way that benefits the person doing the guilting.
- **Diverting**. Bringing the conversation back to yourself constantly through the use of anecdotes and stories or always one-upping them with your own experiences.
- **Grilling**. Pushing for information or clarity to the point where they feel like they have to share information they may not actually feel comfortable sharing.
- **Fixing**. This is a common one. Going straight to fixing and trying to solve the problem rather than listening empathetically can feel very invalidating. If you have agreed to problem-solve together, that's a different story. Fixing is about going straight there with no time to sit in the experience or the feeling.
- **Diagnosis aka 'therapy speak'**. Using diagnostic criteria or therapeutic jargon to name their behaviour and describe why they are the way they are e.g. instead of addressing selfishness, saying, 'You're such a narcissist, it's all about you!'.

It's no surprise that these blocks to communication create negativity. They stop you from being able to communicate well because they make you feel defensive, activate you and result in you not feeling seen, heard or understood.

Good communication doesn't block; it seeks to understand and is open and collaborative. Good communication is broken up into two parts; the role of the speaker who is the giver and the role of the listener who is the receiver. Both roles are equally important. Let's explore each of these in more detail, starting with the receiver.

Listening skills

I want you to take a moment and think back to a time where you felt like someone *really* listened to you. When they *really* heard and understood you. How did it feel? What did they do that made you feel that way? Being a good listener is a skill, just like being a good speaker, and it's something we learn. Listening often doesn't get the attention it deserves when communication is discussed but it really should, because anyone who knows the feeling of continuously not being heard or understood and having to say the same thing again, and again, and again knows the pain. There is a big difference between the safety and peace that comes from feeling heard and understood and the frustration that comes from not feeling heard.

The key elements of being a good listener include:

1. **Active listening.** This is a form of listening that requires presence and your full attention. You cannot be multitasking and must be fully engaging in the conversation. It requires attentiveness, openness and a willingness to explore. When you are actively listening, your sole focus is to hear and understand the other person. That means putting yourself in their shoes, reflecting on what you heard, exploring what is coming up and digging a little deeper by asking open questions.
2. **Validating.** This is not agreeing, it is accepting someone else's emotional experience. People often avoid validating because

they think it means they are agreeing. You don't need to agree with someone to validate their emotional experience. Validating is about saying, 'I get it, I hear you, I understand'. Validating is about accepting their perspective. It's about showing you have heard, understood and accepted the experience they are sharing with you. Invalidating, which is what many of us do without realising, denies their emotional experience, often leaving them feeling judged and unheard. A validating statement might sound like, 'I can understand why that would be upsetting' versus an invalidating statement which might be, 'That's not even a big deal. You're so sensitive'.

3. **Asking open questions**. Open questions are questions that do not have a simple 'yes' or 'no' answer. They seek to explore. Open questions can help you to be a more engaged listener by asking how they are feeling, what the experience was like for them and what they need. It might be something like, 'It sounds like it was a really tough day. Is there anything you need from me right now to support you?'

4. **Curiosity**. A really great listener listens to understand, not merely to respond. They listen with curiosity and their goal is simply to gain a better understanding of the conversation and a person's experience in order to be present with them and empathise.

When you are able to actively listen, validate, ask questions and be curious you are setting the conversation up for the best chance of success. I am not saying these things are always easy, of course they're not. If they were I wouldn't need to talk about them here, but they are possible to learn and improve.

On the other side of the listener is the speaker aka the giver. Who in your life would you describe as a great communicator?

What traits or characteristics do they display? Most of us will know someone either personally or professionally who has great speaking skills. Speaking skills like listening skills are learned.

Speaking skills

A great speaker is aware of what they say and also how they say it. The 'how' is incredibly important when it comes to speaking. The way we speak or share information greatly influences the way our words are interpreted and received. Imagine your partner says to you, 'I'm fine'. The words themselves indicate that yes, they are indeed fine, but if you add some attitude to that, maybe an eye roll, well then, the meaning changes entirely.

The key elements when it comes to speaking are:

1. **How you say it.** Your body language, tone, inflection, pace and pitch all affect how your communication is received. How you say what you're saying is very influential. I have spoken to many people who experience autism spectrum disorder (ASD) or have attention deficit and hyperactivity disorder (ADHD) who have shared this is something they find challenging. If this is you please try not to feel discouraged. The 'how' is not the be-all and end-all.

2. **Choose your words carefully.** If you can choose your words with kindness and respect it's a great start. We cannot take back something we've said, nor can we take back the effect of hurtful words, so trying to avoid the damage they can do is very helpful. If you can't say it respectfully, take a break, walk away and give yourself a moment . . . but do not say it. Words hurt, especially when they come from someone you love. This isn't saying you shouldn't be honest, or assertive, or give feedback;

you can do all of those things respectfully; just choose your words wisely and always be respectful.

3. **Less is more.** We humans don't have the capacity to just keep endlessly absorbing information. Conversations aren't lectures. Sometimes when we desperately want to be understood we keep talking and talking to get our point across. Doing this hinders the goal. It's worth practising getting your key point across in about three sentences then taking a pause and allowing the listener to respond. This is critical when having important conversations. If you just keep talking, the listener might miss something vital. Help them out by taking regular pauses and allowing them to reflect back what they've understood and to ask questions.

4. **Use 'I' statements.** This means speaking from your own per-spective or experience and avoiding speaking for the other person, judging, blaming or using any of the other blockers. When you use 'I' statements you are communicating what is going on for you, how you feel and what you need. It might sound like when 'when (X) happened, I felt (X). What I would prefer/like/need/want is (X)'. Speaking in 'I' statements doesn't give you an excuse to say hurtful things. Sometimes people assume because they are speaking in 'I' statements they can say whatever they want because it's 'their truth'. Don't weaponise the process. If it's not respectful, it's not helpful.

Once you've got these skills, put them to good use. You won't do it perfectly every time; don't worry, you're not a machine. It's like building a muscle; every time you lift the weights and practise the skills you get a little bit stronger and a little bit better. We are not seeking perfection here. We are simply seeking progress.

Now, those speaking and listening skills are good for pretty much any relationship in your life, however in intimate relationships things tend to be more complex, sensitive and difficult to navigate, so there are a few more things to keep in mind.

How to have the hard conversations

We need to have the hard conversations. We need to talk about how we feel when intimacy declines. We need to talk about feeling let down because your partner forgot something important. We need to talk about money, our goals, dreams, fears, insecurities and desires. If we don't, we risk our desires never being fulfilled, we risk not having our needs met or our dreams and goals honoured. Here are a few tips for when you need to have a hard or uncomfortable conversation.

- **Willingness.** The first thing is to see these conversations not as something scary, but rather as opportunities to understand one another better.
- **Timing.** Choose a time where you are not rushing off to do something else, you're not overly tired or stressed and can actually take the time to talk it out. It can be helpful to ask your partner when they have time for a chat in advance so you can both set some time aside.
- **Check in.** Start with a check in around how much capacity you each have in the moment. If it's clear you are both tired, overwhelmed and stressed, postpone the conversation, or if you must chat, be especially gentle with one another.
- **Connect first.** Take a moment to connect before discussing anything serious. That might mean having a chat about your day, sharing a laugh or just having a meal or coffee together and catching up before launching into the topic you want to discuss.

131

The more connected you are, the better the chances are of the conversation going well.

- **Lead with curiosity.** Try to keep an open mind and be curious about your partner/s' thoughts and feelings. Maintaining a sense of curiosity will help you to better understand their position or perspective.
- **Speak in 'I' statements.** Speak for yourself, not for your partner/s. 'I' statements allow you to speak from your own perspective and share what is happening for you and how you are feeling without blaming or criticising. You can use 'I' statements to describe your experience, how you are feeling, and what you need.
- **Stay present.** Stay in the here and now and try not to bring up past situations to prove your point.
- **Know what activates you.** We all have things that activate us. It might be a tone of voice, certain words, behaviours or actions. When you're aware of the things that activate you, you can be prepared and have strategies in place.
- **Take a break.** If you start to become activated or overwhelmed, take a pause, practise self-soothing and then come back together after an agreed amount of time to continue the conversation.
- **Feedback.** Seek feedback after the conversation ends and things have settled to determine how each of you managed it, how it felt and if there are any areas for improvement in the future.

The truth is no-one is a perfect communicator all the time. Even me, a therapist who teaches this stuff, still messes up sometimes! In the end, it's not about perfection, it's about progress. It's about doing your best as often as you can and apologising and trying to improve when you get it wrong. Getting better at communication is like building a muscle; you have to practise, you have to train and you have to actually test it out with heavier and heavier weights aka more uncomfortable or challenging topics. You try, you fail, but you try, try, try again. That's how you get better. That's how you become a good communicator. By learning, making mistakes, improving and then messing it up all over again.

Summary

- Disconnection starts with the words unspoken and through avoiding conflict rather than having the hard conversations.

- We avoid having hard conversations for lots of reasons: people-pleasing, conflict avoidance, fear of creating issues or being too much and trying to protect our partner/s' feelings. All of these avoidance strategies result in disconnection.

- Blocks to communication ruin connection. They include assumptions, talking over each other, not being present and actually listening, judging, guilt-tripping, diverting the focus back to you, grilling for more information, and going straight to fixing or diagnosing.

- Good communication is broken up into two parts: the role of the speaker who is the giver and the role of the listener who is the receiver. Both roles are equally important.

- The key elements of a good listener are active listening (being present and engaging in the conversation fully), validating, asking open questions and leading with curiosity.

- The key elements of a good speaker are being aware of your body language, tone, inflection, pace and pitch, choosing your words wisely, being succinct and using 'I' statements.

- To navigate a hard conversation you want to first choose the right time, check in, connect with one another, lead with curiosity, speak in 'I' statements, stay present, be aware of what activates you, take a break if needed, check in afterwards to see how it went, and exchange feedback.

Activity

Reflect upon the listener and speaker skills. Ask yourself:

- Which of the speaker skills am I good at? Which do I need to improve?

- Which of the listener skills am I good at? Which do I need to improve?

- What do I need when I become activated in a hard conversation?

- What could my partner/s do if I am activated that would help in those moments?

- Have I asked my partner/s what they need in those moments?

9
Clean Fighting

How to fight clean, not dirty

I'll never forget one of the first things my lecturer said when I started studying relationship therapy. 'Sooner or later, your partner is going to get annoying no matter how much you love them.'

'Truth,' I thought.

Regardless of how much we love each other, people can get annoying and frustrating. We all have issues, fights and arguments. We all have challenges that never seem to get resolved and just go round and round in circles. The reality is that arguments or fights are normal and, in fact, healthy. They give us a chance to air our differences, unpack what is really going on, share how we are feeling and connect.

Arguments, when done right, can actually be good for relationships! They can lead you towards more connection and an improved ability to navigate issues. The problem is many of us were not taught how to argue productively. We may not have been taught how to communicate our needs, to navigate differences and to receive feedback without taking it personally. This is what we will explore in this chapter. You will learn the common ways we make things worse, and how to deal with conflict in a productive way. Best of all, you will learn how to fight clean, not dirty.

Your fights about the dishes are not *really* about the dishes. Arguments are rarely about what we think they are. They are not about the surface-level issue; they are about deeper problems such as not feeling like a priority, feeling taken for granted, let down or disappointed. They might be about not feeling wanted or desired. They might be about feeling like your partner always puts their needs before yours, and like you're not important. They might be about feeling like you do more than your fair share around the house. They might be about not feeling seen, heard, valued, accepted or appreciated.

According to the Gottman Institute, most fights have underlying goals, values, dreams and beliefs driving them even if you are focused on a surface-level issue like the dishes.[1] The first thing we need to do, therefore, is understand *why* you feel the way you do. Your thoughts and feelings drive the way you respond so before we learn to fight clean, we need to explore how you can reflect upon what is driving your stance. When a fight, issue or argument comes up, pause and ask yourself:

- Do I have any beliefs, values, goals or dreams which are connected to how I feel about this issue?
- Do I have any past experiences or memories that might be influencing how I feel about this issue?
- Do I have any fears that are influencing how I feel about this issue?

By doing this, you are better able to understand what is driving the way you are thinking, feeling and responding.

Dirty fighting

Fighting dirty is when you're fighting to win. It's about you, not about the relationship. It's about getting your point across, about being right and about making sure your partner/s agree with you rather than letting them have their perspective. Dirty fights usually have one or more of the following:

- **Offending from the 'victim position'.** The term which was coined by author Pia Mellody refers to the process of attacking from the place of victimhood.[2] It can involve guilt-tripping, blaming, or manipulation to make yourself the victim in order to avoid taking responsibility for your part in issues. This isn't necessarily intentional. Some people learned in childhood that playing the victim got them what they needed and they therefore continue to do it in their adult relationships.
- **Defensiveness.** When you are defensive, you are quick to perceive everything as an attack so you therefore deny, deflect or project in order to avoid taking accountability. When you are defensive, there is no space for feedback, there is no space for your partner/s' experience; there is only space for your victimhood . . . which does nothing for the relationship.
- **One-upping.** One-upping is the process of trying to gain the advantage over your partner/s by saying something to trump their experience. It sounds like, 'Well, I may have done this, but *you* did that.' Again, as per above, it is a way of avoiding being accountable. You may be noticing a theme here!
- **Self-righteousness.** This is when you think your beliefs, thoughts, values, emotions, experiences and needs are superior

to your partner/s'. This leads you to engage from a place of perceived superiority and does not put you in a position to negotiate or compromise because you're coming from the position of being 'better than'.

- **Criticism**. When you are critical of your partner and make hurtful remarks it's not surprising that they will respond with defensiveness. Criticism is often an attack on your partner/s' personality or character.
- **Contempt**. A lack of respect for your partner can often be displayed through contempt. It might be eye rolling, a dismissive and critical attitude towards them and/or general dislike. Contempt is absolutely toxic to relationships and according to the Gottman Institute is one of the biggest predictors of divorce.[3]
- **Stonewalling**.[4] This is when you withdraw in order to avoid conflict and shut down the conversation. You might simply not respond, or remove yourself from the situation. Stonewalling is different to 'taking space'. When you take space you communicate that you are overwhelmed and need a moment; stonewalling on the other hand has an element of control to it. It's when you refuse to engage in order to control the dialogue.
- **Personalising**. Personalising is when we make ourselves the central point in the narrative even if something has nothing to do with us. Personalising makes everything about you, when it's not. If you tend to personalise, you might make a huge deal about something going on with your partner that has nothing to do with you which then takes the attention away from them.

You might have noticed that in almost every dirty fighting strategy, there is an avoidance of accountability and making things personal.

There is a pattern of shifting blame and responsibility, being the victim and making everything someone else's fault. This is what we need to shift in order to fight clean.

Clean fighting

Fighting clean involves being able to step outside of yourself as the sole focus. It means moving away from just considering your needs and your experiences and thinking about what is in the best interests of the relationship. To fight clean we need to stop being so 'me' focused and become more 'us' focused. This goes hand in hand with emotional regulation. We can all become activated in arguments. This makes it very difficult to manage our responses, therefore learning to self-soothe and regulate our emotions is vital.

Managing your emotional responses in conflict is not easy. To this day, even though I have been working on it for years, I still struggle to manage my emotional responses. I still have moments where I stuff up, get frustrated, shut down and become self-righteous. I'm human. This isn't about perfection, it's about progress and effort.

Dialectical behaviour therapy (DBT) has a range of tools which have been found to be effective in managing distressing emotions. One of my favourites is ACCEPTS which stands for:[5]

- **Activities**. Try doing an activity that takes your full attention e.g. going for a run, calling a friend or doing a task around the home.
- **Contributing**. Contribute to another person's life, so fully engage with someone else, not the person you are activated by. It could be a friend, family member, child or even a pet.
- **Comparisons**. Comparisons are generally unhelpful, however, in this case we can use them as a form of encouragement. We can

remind ourselves of other challenging times we have experienced that we have managed to navigate. Doing this will give ourselves a boost to help us get through whatever is happening in the moment.

- **Emotions.** Do something that will help you to change your emotional state. For me, my go-to is funny raccoon videos on YouTube! Watching silly raccoons always, without fail, helps me shift my mood. What works for you? It could be speaking to someone in particular, watching something or listening to something.
- **Pushing away.** Use methods like visualisations, meditation and breath work to help you push away the feeling.
- **Thoughts.** Our thoughts significantly contribute to how we feel, so actively working on redirecting or challenging unhelpful or negative thoughts can help you to self-soothe and regulate your emotions.
- **Sensations.** Try focusing on something that will help you tune into the sensations in your body. You could eat something sweet or spicy or have a cold shower.

—

When it comes to regulating emotions it's really all about finding what works for you. I often encourage my clients to write a list of things that help them in those moments and put it on their fridge. Then, when it happens and you are dysregulated all you have to do is go and choose something from the list to practise in that moment. Once you have some strategies in place to help with emotional regulation and self-soothing, you can then focus on learning how to fight clean.

The key elements of clean fighting are:

- **Timing.** Choose your time wisely. Sure, sometimes fights will happen out of the blue. Most of the time, though, they don't; they have been festering below the surface and we choose to rumble when we get to a point of being so annoyed we can't possibly hold it in anymore. When you are mindful of timing, you choose to raise an issue with your partner/s at an appropriate time. So this means you are not running out the door, are not too stressed about other things and have some capacity to properly engage in the conversation.
- **Validate.** When it comes to communication, validation is your super power. If you can get good at validating your partner/s' emotional experience and sitting with it, it will without a shadow of a doubt improve your relationship. Validating is *not* agreeing. It is accepting your partner/s' emotional experience. It is saying, 'I hear you, I get it', and stepping into their shoes.
- **Seek to understand.** The goal should be to understand your partner/s' perspective as best you can. Like with validating, you do not need to agree. You are simply trying to understand. You can do this by staying curious and remembering regardless of how long you have been together you cannot read their mind (unless you actually can? Are you a psychic? Is that real?). Ask questions.
- **Assume the best.** Try to assume the best rather than the worst. Our minds are wired to be more inclined to the negative so it's difficult especially if you've been having issues for a while. But by assuming the best we set ourselves up to be more open to the positive.
- **Lead with respect.** You each have a right to your own thoughts, feelings and emotions. Leading with respect honours their experience and yours at the same time. It allows for differences of opinion, without dismissing individual feelings, or experiences.

- **Take space mindfully.** If you become activated or emotionally overwhelmed and need to take space, communicate this to your partner. Tell them what you need (space) and for how long before you take it and then agree on a time to come back together and discuss the issue. If we just take space without any agreement about when we will return to the conversation, it can provoke anxiety in the other person.

- **Two opposing things can be true.** Your reality is subjective. Your interpretation of the world and experiences are shaped by your beliefs, values, memories, emotions and perspectives. This is why two people can have the same experience and feel totally different about it. This is why we need to remember two things can be true at once. Just because you think one way doesn't make it the only way or the only truth.

- **Equality.** You are equal and you need to argue as such. Do not use your position or privilege to win. It doesn't matter who does more of what, who earns more money, or anything else that makes you think it's okay to one-up your partner. If you're not leading with equality, then it's not fair and it's not respectful.

- **Accountability.** The most important part of clean fighting in my opinion is accountability. You need to take responsibility for your part in the issue or argument. In reality, other than in cases of abuse, all issues are shared. We each bring something to the table so be accountable for your part. This makes you vulnerable, yes, but if we want a partner to be vulnerable and own their part then we need to do the same. Leading with vulnerability, honesty and a willingness to be imperfect creates safety. When you do this, others will feel safe to reciprocate.

- **Your partner is not the enemy, the issue is.** Stop fighting each other and start working together to brainstorm solutions. Focus on the issue at hand, not who is to blame.

- **Apologise and forgive.** We all mess up sometimes and say things we later regret. When this happens, apologise. Take accountability, name what you did that you regret and make a commitment not to do it again. When your partner does this, try to forgive them and let it go. Holding onto it and punishing them later for the way they messed up when they have apologised and made change isn't fair and damages trust.
- **Give and receive feedback.** One way we can get better at navigating conflict is by giving and receiving feedback. That means after conflict has happened and has been resolved actually talking to one another about how you each navigated the argument, how it felt, and what could be improved in the future.

When we fight clean and practise the above strategies, arguments can bring us closer together. They can make the relationship stronger and help build trust. When we fight clean, we are truly showing up. We are saying, 'I value you', 'I respect you' and 'you are important' and this is where true partnership, vulnerability and safety thrive. I mean, how good does that sound? All we need to do is get out of our ego and move into a space of collaboration. *All* we need to do? Yeah, I know I make it sound easy!

One of the reasons people find it hard is because when we've had issues for a while, we can find ourselves in something known as 'negative sentiment override'.[6] This term was coined by Drs John and Julie Gottman and it refers to how negative thoughts and feelings about your partner build up over time and make you more likely to interpret their words, behaviours and actions in a negative light.

When you're stuck in negative sentiment override, you are wired to receive your partner/s in a negative way even if what they are saying or doing is neutral. It's imperative therefore to redirect your attention. They could be working on improving their communication, or regulating their emotions, or navigating conflict. Even though they may be making significant process, you simply can't see it because you are stuck in negative sentiment override.

To get out of negative sentiment override you need to consciously look for things that *are* working, things they are doing right and things you appreciate about them. One way you can do this is by creating a daily ritual to focus on what you appreciate about one another. You need to be intentional about looking for things that are working. This will help to actively shift your focus. When done every day, it will help move you out of negative sentiment override.

To get out of negative sentiment override you need to consciously look for things that *are* working, things they are doing right and things you appreciate about them.

Of course, it's not just about what you pay attention to, you need to also treat each other well, communicate well and show love, but even with those things if you are not choosing to look for what's working, you can miss it.

Summary

- Most arguments are *not* about the surface-level issues. They are about underlying hopes, dreams and fears. They are driven by underlying feelings. Most arguments are about not feeling like a priority, feeling taken for granted, not feeling wanted or desired, or not feeling considered, cared for or important.

- Fighting dirty is when you're fighting to win. It's about you, not about the relationship. It's about getting your point across, about being right and about making sure your partner/s agree with you rather than letting them have their perspective. Examples of fighting dirty include offending from the victim position, defensiveness, one-upping, self-righteousness, personalising, criticism, displaying contempt and stonewalling.

- Fighting clean involves being able to step outside of yourself as the sole focus. It means moving away from just considering your needs and your experiences, and thinking about what is in the best interests of the relationship. To fight clean, we need to stop being so 'me' focused and start being more 'us' focused.

- In order to fight clean you must: choose your timing wisely, validate, seek to understand, assume the best, lead with respect, take space mindfully, accept different realities, create equality, take accountability, apologise, forgive and be open to feedback.

- When we fight clean and practise these strategies, arguments can bring us closer. They can make the relationship stronger and they can actually build trust. When we fight clean, we are truly showing up to the relationship.

Activity

Have a think and answer the following questions:

- How have you fought dirty in the past? What effect did it have on your relationship?

- How did it feel when someone fought dirty with you?

- What are your go-to self-soothing strategies when you become emotionally dysregulated during conflict?

- What elements of clean fighting do you want to work on improving?

10

Bend and Mend

What it means to bend in relationships and mend after ruptures

Great relationships aren't always sunshine and rainbows. Hopefully, you've taken that much from this book if you've made it this far! They can be challenging. They require us to show up, grow, embrace discomfort and be less self-centred. We have to put someone else's needs on the same level as ours and that can be incredibly annoying at times. We need to desire our partner/s' happiness as much as our own. We need to truly want the best for them and, as a result, challenge ourselves to show up as the best partner we can be in each and every moment. What that looks like will depend on the structure of your own particular relationship. Whatever your scenario, we must all acknowledge the areas we need to grow, and do our best.

The ability to 'bend and mend' is one of the greatest tools in your arsenal when it comes to navigating this process. 'Bending' simply means to be able to adapt, change and grow – both individually and together. We need to have the freedom to grow in order to be able to thrive in relationship. 'Mending', on the other hand, means to come back together and reconnect after moments of disconnection that result in feelings of distance. When you can effectively bend and mend you have the power to create a relationship built on resilience, freedom and growth.

Bend

There's no denying there's discomfort in disagreeing, in not being on the same page, and in feeling like you're incompatible. But this discomfort should be embraced, not avoided. It can be uncomfortable to bend, to compromise and give in because most of us are taught to always fight to win. We are taught that by bending we are somehow sacrificing. Often we are so self-focused we don't stop to think about how much we even care about the thing we are fighting over. Are you fighting to win when you don't even care that much? Do you just not want to sacrifice? Or maybe you don't believe you should have to sacrifice at all?

Here's a concept that makes for a good middle ground: *who cares most, wins.* I am willing to compromise and negotiate a lot of things when I assess how much I actually care. Do I care about where we eat tonight? Not really. But do I care about the dishes being done the same day as they were used? Yes, I certainly do!

In relationships, just as in life, you have to 'pick your battles'. It's easy when one person cares (they win), and the other doesn't (they bend). However, when you *both* care, that's where the fun starts. It signifies the issue at hand is important. It shows you need to give it time and attention, unpack it and explore it. Do this by investigating what the argument or issue is *really* about. Start by asking yourself:

- Do I have any beliefs or values which are connected with my stance?
- Are there any past experiences which are connected with how I feel in the present?
- Do I have any dreams, goals, or fears connected to my stance?
- Do I feel like I have to give up or change a core part of me?

Then, ask your partner/s:

- What makes this issue so important to you?
- Do you have any dreams, goals, or fears connected to your stance?
- Are there any past experiences which are connected with how you feel in the present?

When we struggle to bend it's usually because we sense some sort of threat. We fear that if we bend or compromise, we will be sacrificing a dream, goal or need and feel the urge to protect ourselves. In some cases where you both deeply care about your position, this is totally valid, but the key is to try to keep those issues to a minimum.

When you find yourself struggling to bend, see it as an opportunity to dig a little deeper and explore what fears may be present. One of the reasons many people struggle to bend is they feel as if compromising might threaten their independence. Sometimes we feel it's a risk to take on board another person's perspective because we might lose ourselves or somehow sacrifice our needs. So instead, we unconsciously use coping mechanisms and what we call 'cognitive biases'. These can include:

- **Projection.** Putting uncomfortable thoughts, feelings, emotions or insecurities onto your partner/s rather than owning them yourself.

- **Discounting the positive.** Minimising the positive aspects of the relationship and giving more value and attention to the behaviours, situations or issues you perceive as negative.
- **Jumping to conclusions.** Filling in the blanks and making assumptions with minimal evidence rather than asking questions and believing your partner/s.
- **Catastrophising.** Blowing things way out of proportion and making a bigger deal than is necessary.
- **Emotional reasoning.** Taking the way we feel as evidence and believing it reflects the reality of the situation. In other words, using feelings as factual evidence, when they are not.
- **Shoulds.** Creating binary ideas and expectations around how people or things 'should' be.
- **Personalisation.** Thinking everything has something to do with you. Making yourself the central point in a narrative that may have nothing to do with you. This results in you being very affected by circumstances out of your control.
- **Negativity bias.** The tendency to hyper-focus on the negative. This then affects your psychological state.
- **Confirmation bias.** Only seeing or paying attention to information and signs that confirm what you already believe. New information only serves to deepen your commitment to already established beliefs.

We all use these sorts of cognitive biases and defence mechanisms from time to time. Mostly they're unconscious, however unconscious or not, they still create issues. When you find yourself using cognitive biases, or are given feedback that suggests you may be using them, think about the validity of that feedback. Are you wedded to a certain idea simply because it's what you were taught as a child?

Don't try to stop arguing. It's not about avoiding arguments. Research tells us that it's not so much about *how much* you argue or *what you argue about* but rather *how you repair*.[1] The way you repair is incredibly important as this is how you reconnect. There will be many moments of disconnection and reconnection in relationships so learning how to repair well is your magic medicine.

Research tells us that it's not so much about *how much* you argue or *what you argue about* but rather *how you repair*.

Mend

If you follow any relationship therapy content on social media you will have no doubt heard the term 'rupture and repair'. It comes from Drs John and Julie Gottman's research. In essence, a 'rupture' is something that causes a loss of connection in a relationship, while a 'repair' is an attempt to restore that connection. Experiencing ruptures in relationships is inevitable. We all have disagreements, issues, arguments, conflicts, differences of opinions, moments of letting one another down and simply stuffing up. The aim is not to avoid ruptures altogether but rather learning how to manage and repair them. Repairs are any attempt at re-establishing connection following a rupture.[2] They might include:

- **Apologising.** Taking accountability and apologising for something you did that hurt your partner/s.
- **Changing your mind and agreeing.** If you are arguing, changing your mind and agreeing with your partner/s is an effective attempt to repair.
- **Expressing care.** You might say nice things, express compliments or do something to show you care.

- **Compromise.** You might work together to find a compromise.
- **Exploration.** You might attempt to unpack the argument and explore what is going on and why it's worth resolving it.
- **Humour.** You might attempt to shift the topic by using humour.
- **Agreements.** You might make commitments as to how you will change your behaviour or do something differently in the future.
- **Empathy.** You might try stepping into your partner/s' shoes and understanding their perspective. This might be through expressing compassion, empathy and understanding.
- **Sharing.** You might share how you are feeling and what is happening for you in an attempt to feel closer.

When one person makes a repair attempt, the other person has three options. They can either accept and respond to the repair attempt; they can reject it; or they can totally miss it. How someone responds plays a big role in the effectiveness of the repair attempt.

But it's a two-way street. We need to be open to receiving a repair attempt in order for it to work. Research has found that not all repair attempts are given the same value. Cognitive and rational repair attempts like problem-solving and compromise tend to be less effective than focusing on re-establishing emotional closeness. Repair attempts that concentrate on empathy and connection also tend to be more effective.[3] Taking responsibility was found to be one of the most effective repair attempts, as was demonstrating understanding and care, and even taking a pause and redirecting.

Try to explore how you like to repair after conflict. Ask your partner/s what works for them. Some people respond really well to redirection and humour while for others that can feel invalidating. Learning what works for your partner/s is like learning how they want to be loved. You will be far more effective in your repair attempts if you know what feels good, sincere and helpful.

How to repair

Repairing involves reconnecting, re-establishing closeness and moving through and beyond the issue at hand. 'Cognitive repairs' focus on problem-solving and unpacking the issue. Examples of how you might attempt a cognitive-focused repair include:

- Unpacking the situation and trying to better understand one another's position in order to come up with a compromise.
- Unpacking why you felt annoyed or upset and exploring ways you could better navigate the issue next time.
- Focusing on potential solutions and going into 'problem-solving mode'.

'Emotionally focused' repairs are about reconnecting, and showing understanding and empathy. Examples of how you might attempt a more emotionally focused repair include:

- Focusing on understanding and trying to put yourself in the other person's shoes. This allows you to hold space and show compassion for their experience.
- Being vulnerable and sharing your experience and feelings to enable your partner to understand what's happening for you and to allow them to show up for you.
- Providing reassurance that you are there for them, they are important to you and you are on the same team.
- Showing affection and attempting to become closer and more connected physically.
- Apologising and taking responsibility for your part in the issue.

Becoming aware of how you attempt to repair and also what your partner/s do can help you to better understand when they are trying to reconnect. Sometimes, the attempt might be subtle and if we don't know what we're looking for we'll miss it.

—

It's time we let go. We need to let go of the idea that relationships shouldn't require any effort and accept that like everything else, we get out what we put in. We need to realise that all relationships have lulls and that doesn't mean it's the wrong relationship or the love has died. It just means a little time, attention and energy are required to relight the fire.

We need to let go of the idea that relationships shouldn't require any effort and accept that like everything else, we get out what we put in.

In the end, there is no perfect relationship. Everyone is different, therefore the type of relationship they have needs to reflect that, whether that means monogamous, non-monogamous or just casually dating. We are not always right, and fighting to be right means the relationship loses. We need to ditch the idea that a relationship or partner/s will complete us because all that does is set us up for unhealthy co-dependence.

Essentially, we need to let go of all the rubbish we unconsciously learned that no longer helps us, and actively relearn the things that do. We need to learn and unlearn in unison. We need to do this in relationship with ourselves, in how we relate to one another and in our sex lives. This is what I have been trying to facilitate on this journey so far.

We've covered what drives how you engage in relationships, explored the typical hurdles in relationship dynamics and discussed some effective methods for overcoming them. Now, we are going to move onto the juicy stuff. Now, finally, we are going to talk about sex! The next part is all about discovering your sexual self and exploring your desires.

Summary

- Bending means to be able to adapt, change and grow both individually and together. To mend is to come back together and reconnect after moments of disconnection that result in feelings of distance.

- The 'who cares the most wins' method is easy to use and goes like this: when one person cares (they win), and the other doesn't (they bend). If you both deeply care about something, and not just about winning, it signifies it is important. It shows you need to unpack it and explore it.

- If we feel it's a risk to take on board another person's perspective or to compromise because we might lose ourselves, we'll quickly utilise coping mechanisms and cognitive biases.

- A 'rupture' is something that causes a loss of connection, while a 'repair' is an attempt to restore that sense of connection.

- Becoming aware of how you attempt to repair and also what your partner/s do can be an incredibly helpful way to be more intentional about repairs.

Activity

How do you repair? Ask yourself and your partner/s the following questions:

- What do you do to stop conflict from escalating?

- What does a repair attempt look like from you? How will your partner/s know if you are trying to repair?

- What repair attempts feel most sincere and helpful?

- Is there anything that helps you to feel better after a rupture?

- How will you know that the repair has been effective? What does it feel like?

PART THREE

ALL ABOUT SEX AND INTIMACY

11

A Modern Sex Education

What were you taught about sex?

Would you believe that sex was barely covered when I studied to be a relationship therapist? When I chose my speciality, I sought out training in the most popular and well-researched areas and was surprised to find that most only briefly discussed sex. I thought this must be an oversight, surely! I began searching for more information and found that no, it wasn't.

The most prominent teaching focused on the friendship within the relationship and suggested if the friendship was good, then the sex would be good too. I became confused because this teaching was well researched and yet it did not align with what I was seeing in my practice, it wasn't what I was seeing in my community and it didn't reflect the experiences I'd had myself.

Many clients would come to me and say, 'We have a great relationship and I love my partner but we don't have sex anymore. What do we do?' It was a good question, but honestly, I had no idea how to answer it. I started to notice a theme: sometimes the more comfortable people became in their relationship, the less libido, desire and passion they would experience. I also heard how many people who have small children just didn't have the capacity for sex anymore, didn't want it anymore, or were completely touched out at the end of the day.

I realised there were big gaps. There was a gap in my knowledge but also a gap in the market because a lot of books written specifically about relationships didn't actually talk about sex. They talked about communication, emotions and connection but left out sex.

The importance of sex will differ from person to person and relationship to relationship. Sex is as important as you feel it is. It's vital to note that however you choose to value sexual intimacy – how much importance or unimportance you place on it – is normal, natural and absolutely okay. I am not saying sex is the be-all and end-all, but it was something I wanted to figure out so I could help my clients. I wanted answers!

In my household growing up, sex was spoken about, not in detail, but it definitely wasn't a taboo subject. It was seen as healthy and natural, yet for some reason I never felt confident, didn't really enjoy it, and I couldn't understand why. It became a roadblock in my relationships. In the early days, the sex would be all hot and spicy and we would get close and comfortable and then . . . *boom*, my desire would vanish. This resulted in great relationships ending because I felt like there was something missing. For me, it was that physical and sexual closeness. I kept thinking it would be different with the next person. But it wasn't.

At the same time, clients I spoke to were experiencing something similar, the only difference was they chose to stay in the relationship and tried to work it out, while I chose to leave and to seek out that missing piece of the puzzle elsewhere. The regularity in which I started to hear about this phenomenon led me on a journey of self-discovery. I sought out information through books, programs and I completed a Masters in Psychosexual Therapy. Over time, I learned a lot, and I bridged some of those gaps.

This part of *All In* is about sharing what I learned through that process. I want to offer you a short re-education on sex and intimacy. Think of is as a modern-day adult sex education class that will teach you all the things that were likely left out of your actual sex education. Hopefully, it will also instil some hope, passion and excitement into your love life.

A sexual re-education

Much of what we think and feel about sex comes from what we learned growing up. In many families, sex is either not discussed at all, or it is spoken about in shameful, judgemental or fearful ways. Even in school, 'sex education' mostly focuses on sexually transmitted infections, how to avoid teenage pregnancy, consent and contraception. Don't get me wrong, this stuff is important, but it's also a slightly fearful and 'sex negative' way of approaching the topic.

While I understand why schools can't necessarily teach pleasure, if the Netflix TV show *Sex Education* has taught me anything it's that knowledge is power and the more sexually empowered we feel, the more confident we will be at navigating these somewhat awkward conversations. So, with that in mind, let's start from the very beginning and explore where your sexual attitudes came from and how they influence your relationship with sex.

The American Psychological Association (APA) describes sexual attitudes as your 'values and beliefs about sexuality. Manifested in a person's individual sexual behaviour, these attitudes are based on family and cultural views about sexuality, on sex education (both formal and informal), and on prior sexual experiences'.[1] Your sexual attitude, also called a 'sexual script', is made up of your beliefs, values, expectations and understanding of yourself as a sexual being. It's not just about sexuality in terms of whom you are attracted to, but the factors that influence how you think about sex and engage in sexual behaviour. Our sexual attitude is created through what we see and hear about sex as well as our sexual experiences.

Let's unpack what makes up your sexual attitude. The goal here isn't necessarily to change it but rather to better understand how it influences the ways you think about and engage in sex.

Values

Your sexual values, like any other values, are the fundamental beliefs that guide what you perceive to be right and wrong or good and bad. They create a basis for the way you express yourself sexually and how you interpret the desires, actions (what they do) and behaviour (how they do it) of others.

These values influence how we behave and how we see ourselves as sexual beings. They also guide how we feel when we see something or are asked to do something that goes against our sexual values. For example, you might value monogamy, or not having sex until the fifth date, or you might be uncomfortable with certain types of sex. Your values might also influence how important or unimportant sexual intimacy is to you.

Expectations

Your sexual expectations are your beliefs about what can, will or should happen and how. Expectations might include beliefs about gender roles, or who should initiate touch or sexual intimacy, the ways you engage in sex, or about how often you should be having sex when you're in a relationship. For example, you might have an expectation of healthy couples having sex at least once a week. This then influences how you think and feel about your sex life if you are *not* having sex once a week.

Experiences

The experiences you've had, especially early sexual ones, influence how you think and feel about sex. If you felt self-conscious or had someone give you negative sexual feedback, this may continue to affect your confidence and influence the sorts of sex you choose to engage in. Experiencing sexual trauma can also have a profound effect.

Developing your sexual identity

If we were shamed, judged or criticised about our sexuality or desires growing up it can lead to shame and sexual 'disembodiment' as an adult. This is what happened to me. It wasn't so much that sex wasn't spoken about, it was, but I didn't see any modelling that resonated with me and that reflected who I felt I was.

I grew up in Sydney's northern suburbs, in an area that was not diverse in any way, shape or form. Heterosexuality was the norm. In high school, I only knew one person who was gay, so it wasn't even on my radar. As a teen, I knew there was something that felt different for me, but I couldn't quite put my finger on what it was. Sometimes I would become overly jealous about certain female friends and get very attached. It just didn't seem to make sense (it does now).

In my twenties, I moved to London to spend more time with my relatives and get some experience out in the big wide world. That time really changed how I knew myself. I became involved in queer culture and attended fabulous LGBTQIA dancing events with my aunt. I was astounded at how at peace I felt.

I remember watching a men's Latin dance competition and feeling at home, like I belonged for the first time in my life. Being in these spaces and having more queer friends began to normalise my own feelings about my sexuality. After developing a very intense crush on a female I slowly began to realise I was queer. I was twenty-nine at the time and it completely rocked me because it challenged everything I knew about myself.

Yes, I admit I had an identity crisis. While I'd always had a feeling, it was buried so deep it came as quite a shock to the system. This began a re-forming of my sexual identity. During this time I feared being sexually inept when it came to women; after all, up until that point I had always been with men. I realised that I needed to work on my sexual self-confidence.

Sexual self-confidence, aka sexual self-esteem, is the feeling of being comfortable and capable of engaging in sex and intimacy in a way that pleases you and your partner/s. It includes the way you perceive yourself and your body, how you express your sexuality, the partner/s you choose, how you communicate and how you view yourself as a sexual being. Having low sexual self-esteem may result in us not feeling comfortable naked, not expressing ourselves during sex or avoiding sexual intimacy altogether.

On the other hand, having higher levels of sexual self-esteem is associated with greater sexual satisfaction, being more comfortable in our bodies and the freedom to express our desires, wants and needs. It is also associated with greater relationship satisfaction.

Increasing your sexual self-confidence starts with getting comfortable with *you*.

How do you build sexual self-confidence?

Get comfortable with your body

This one is easier said than done. Body image is complex, and I am not going to pretend that a few paragraphs in this book are going to result in a quick fix. However, it's important to address it because body image plays a big part in our sexual self-confidence.

We've only got one body so you'd think we would all cherish it, yet so many of us spend an inordinate amount of time judging it for how it looks without really appreciating all it does. I mean, you are breathing right now without having to even think about it. Isn't that incredible?

If you are someone who struggles with their body image there are a few things that you can do:

- Start paying attention to the way you think about your body and shift the focus of your thoughts to the things you like about it, what it can do and how it feels, rather than how it looks.
- Take care of your body. This means eating well and exercising. Building a better relationship with your body isn't just mental, it's physical, and it's achieved through the choices you make. Taking care of your body and treating it with love will help you to increase appreciation for it and improve how you think and feel about it. Treat your body like a best friend who has had your back since the moment you were born.
- Try using things like clothing, lighting or props that make you feel sexy. If you feel uncomfortable being naked with the lights on, that's okay. Find ways to play with the lighting that help you feel more comfortable. Perhaps use lamps, candles or fairy lights. And turn off any bright fluoro lights!

Ultimately, you don't have to absolutely love how your body looks to be confident – very few people do – but it is helpful to explore how your relationship with your body influences the way you feel about and engage in sex.

Work through any sexual shame

Sexual shame is a feeling of embarrassment, guilt or self-judgement about the thoughts or feelings you have about sex, the sorts of fantasies you enjoy, the things you desire and the ways you engage in sex and sex play. Sexual shame influences whether we achieve sexual satisfaction and can also play a part in sexual dysfunction. Sexual shame often prevents us from feeling comfortable in our bodies, with our partner/s and experiencing our desires. It can make us feel inadequate and disgusted with ourselves and can negatively affect our mental health, relationships and self-esteem.[2]

A lot of people carry some sort of sexual shame. This is because many of us have been raised in cultures that don't talk about sex, but rather judge it. Many cultures ostracise people for their sexuality and sexual interests. While the degree of interest in sex will vary from person to person (we will explore libido and desire in the following chapters), experiencing sexual urges is completely normal. Think about it, if it didn't feel good and we didn't have sexual drive there would literally be no people. We wouldn't procreate and humanity wouldn't exist!

The problem is that many cultures focus on only one aspect of sex and that is procreation. We live in an era that has seen liberation in sex, gender and sexuality in countless ways, yet we still carry the sexual shame of generations past. The way to work through sexual shame is firstly to acknowledge and accept that you may be carrying it around. Accept that it may be affecting the way you feel about sex, your sexuality or gender. Try writing it down in order to make sense of it. Explore where its origins lie, what social messages you may have heard that led to you feeling it, and then show yourself compassion.

Explore any beliefs or values that may be contributing to this feeling and ask yourself if they still hold true for you. Then, check in with your thoughts. Are there any negative ideas that need to be challenged? Processing shame is a gradual exercise that involves moving into acceptance where you once may have been in judgement. It's about freeing yourself and letting go of the idea that you need to be any different to how you are.

Find some support to work through any sexual trauma

While this topic could really be a whole book in itself, I want to take a moment to briefly explore the effect trauma can have on sex, desire and libido. Those affected by sexual trauma often experience a sense of 'disembodiment'.[3] This is when we disconnect from our bodies and physiological experience during sex, even when we feel safe. We may want to be present and enjoy ourselves, but we find ourselves 'checking out'.

Becoming disembodied stops up from being able to fully experience the present and often results in the inability to orgasm or ejaculate because we're not fully there for the experience. It's kind of like sexual disassociation.

Trauma can also influence how safe we feel with our partner/s, our level of drive and libido, as well as the sorts of things that turn us on and off. If this resonates with you and you would like to access further support, please reach out to a therapist or contact one of the support services listed at the end of the book.

Challenge unhelpful thoughts

Much of our sexual self-confidence is in our heads. Performance anxiety or unhelpful thoughts can result in us being unable to get our bodies to do what we want. You might struggle with premature ejaculation, have difficulty getting an erection or find yourself faking orgasms. Of course, there can also be medical or physiological reasons, but more often it's connected to our thinking patterns. It's often connected with difficulties being fully present in our bodies because we're stuck in our heads.

We need to start paying attention to our thoughts and challenging those that stop us from being present in order to enjoy our sexual encounters. Do you have any repetitive thoughts about sex that are making you anxious, insecure, or unable to be present? Take a moment to notice the thoughts you have about sex. Do you have any fears? Do you have any insecurities that arise right before you get naked? Write them down and challenge them. By challenging them I don't mean you have to flip them into a positive, I just mean asking yourself, 'Is this true?', 'Is this reasonable?', 'Is this likely?' and 'Does it actually matter?'. You might even ask yourself, 'What is the best-case scenario? What is the worst-case scenario? What is the most-likely-case scenario?'[4]

Become aware of what is influencing you

Porn culture has done a real disservice to having satisfying sex. It's created this image of sex being a 'wham bam thank you ma'am' kind of deal. Porn and sections of the media have taught us to focus on the end game, on orgasm and ejaculation, rather than pleasure, closeness, connection, fun and excitement. Sex doesn't need to be like porn. In fact, it's going to be a whole lot better when you move away from the stereotypes that porn perpetuates and focus instead on pleasure.

Learn your craft, but learn from reputable sources. It might sound a little weird, but being a good lover is learned. It's not learned from porn, it's learned through connections with your partner/s. It begins with understanding our bodies and the science behind pleasure.

Would you go into a big presentation at work completely unprepared and with no idea of the topic you're going to be talking about? Of course you wouldn't. So why is sex any different? We just expect we should be great at it because we reach puberty and want it, but even if you know what you like, learning a partner/s' body and their likes and dislikes is a process of exploration . . . and a fun one when you're comfortable and open.

Discovering your likes and dislikes

Discovering your sexual likes and dislikes is an ongoing and enjoyable process which changes as you age. The things you like as a 25-year-old will likely be very different to what you enjoy at fifty.

It's time to explore! This might mean trying different positions, toys and scenarios with your partner/s, or it might be something more individual like self-pleasure. Self-pleasure or masturbation allows you to explore your body without the pressure of having another person present. It can be a great way to learn what you like and also what gives you the ick! Working out your likes, dislikes and preferences will help you to feel more comfortable and increase your sexual self-confidence.

Exploring your erotic side

Eroticism is the exploration of our inner urges, desires, thoughts and dreams. It's the anticipation and tension that builds in our minds and bodies. We are going to go into this in more detail in Chapter 14 but for now, have a think about your fantasies and urges, and what builds anticipation and sexual tension for you. Much of what makes sex good happens in our minds and has little to do with the physical act itself – it's more about how we *think* about what's happening than what is *actually* happening.

Learning to communicate your wants, desires and boundaries

You know what almost always leads to better sex? Talking about it! It's not a sexy answer, I know, but it's true. For a lot of people, sex is a taboo topic. This often leads to a disappointing sex life. But if we don't talk about it how can we improve it? We can't assume our partner/s know what we want, like or what turns us on, and similarly, we can't assume we know their wants, turn ons or likes without actually asking them.

If we want to have great sex, we need to be able to talk about it. Talking about sex can be awkward, so learning to navigate those conversations is critical. If you have a partner and can talk about all this stuff before getting into the bedroom, then that's great. Sit down, have a cup of tea and discuss how you want to spice things up – things you want to try or things that turn you on. Then leave the conversation and let it settle. You don't have to go straight from the conversation to sex as that can feel really forced, so leave it for a day, forget about it and let it all come naturally the next time you're intimate.

If we want to have great sex, we need to be able to talk about it.

Use your voice to teach your partner what you like. A simple change in tone and inflection can shift an instruction from direct to sexy. Giving feedback during sex through verbal and physical signals helps your partner to get to know your body. If you don't like something, redirect them elsewhere. If you do like something, tell them.

How do you turn down sex or communicate that you're not in the mood? We all know how vulnerable initiating sex can make us feel, so try to be sensitive if you turn it down. Of course, it's okay to do so, but the act of saying 'not tonight' isn't the part that upsets people, it's *how* it is said and how it makes them feel. Start by acknowledging their initiation, even if you couldn't possibly imagine why they feel like sex in that moment. *Turn down the sexual invitation, not your partner.* Context is helpful so explaining how you're not in the mood will help your partner/s not to take the rejection so personally.

Be present and tune into your body

Ultimately, if you want to fully enjoy sex and feel sexually self-confident, you need to be present in your body and not off in some faraway land. The practice of presence requires mindfulness and awareness. Cultivating presence and mindfulness can be done through practices such as mindful breathing. Mindful breathing involves tuning in and concentrating on the breath and bringing all your attention to the body while you focus on filling and emptying your lungs. You might like to try a 'body scan' where you sit quietly with your eyes closed and just shift your attention to the various parts of your body. Notice how this feels, including any tension, warmth or other sensations you may be experiencing.

By practising mindfulness and body awareness you will learn to be present and focus your attention on your body. This is an activity you could do together or by yourself. Being able to be fully present, in body and mind, is the ultimate goal. When you mix these ingredients together it helps you to build sexual self-confidence and feel comfortable in yourself.

—

Okay, now let's talk about some of the realities in long-term relationships, so you don't find yourself with unrealistic expectations that don't come to fruition and then unnecessarily shatter all your hopes and dreams. People often ask me what's 'normal' when it comes to sex and relationships. Their questions often centre around what is the average number of times that people in happy long-term relationships have sex, rather than about the quality of that sex.

The media and Western culture have promoted somewhat unrealistic expectations, so before we explore how to inject more passion and desire into your sex life, I first want to investigate the reality of sex in long-term relationships because the truth is it's not about quantity, it's about quality. We also need to unpack what makes your sex life 'good enough'.

Is good enough sex, in fact, good enough?

In all relationships, it's incredibly common to have lulls in sex, libido and desire. If we believe sex should be great all the time, it can negatively influence the way we see ourselves, our partner/s and the relationship itself. The reality is about 45 per cent of relationships will experience some sort of sexual dysfunction at some point in time.[5]

What is sexual dysfunction, I hear you ask? Well, it's really anything that creates challenges around sex and gets in the way of you wanting or enjoying sex and physical intimacy. It could have something to do with desire or libido; it could be difficulty coming to ejaculation or orgasm; it could be pain during intercourse; or it could be that you experience adverse side effects to medications that affect your sex drive. Honestly, it could be so many different things which is why it is so common and, yes, normal! This is why when I talk about sex, it's important for each individual and relationship to have a basis for what is 'good enough' for all those times when it might not be mind-blowing.

Something that really resonated with me is the 'Good Enough Sex Model' developed by the American psychologists Michael Metz and Barry McCarthy.[6] Now, before you put down the book thinking, 'I want to have *great* sex not merely "good enough" sex', bear with me! We'll get there in the following chapters, but let's first lay down some ground work.

The model developed by Metz and McCarthy explores twelve principles of 'good enough' sex with a focus on pleasure and intimacy. The model is grounded in creating a safe environment where we have realistic expectations that actually set us up to experience better sex. The twelve principles suggest sex and intimacy enhance relationships and help people sustain connection through life's inevitable challenges. The model encourages us to embrace our sexual selves and work on dismantling any barriers that may get in the way of having positive sexual experiences. It explores how sex and relationship satisfaction are intertwined and through deepening our emotional intimacy, we can have better sexual intimacy.

The model highlights that as we go through life, we all experience health challenges as our bodies change with age. It's normal for these changes to influence our sex drive and how we engage in sex, and it may mean we need to make adjustments and explore new ways to connect sexually.

The purpose is pleasure, not to get to 'the end'. Bringing the focus back to pleasure takes the pressure off and will produce a far more enjoyable experience. It's not going to be mind-blowing every time. The quality of sex you have will vary and that's okay. Sex serves many functions, including facilitating an intimate and pleasurable experience; managing stress and anxiety; maintaining a feeling of closeness; nurturing the relationship; building self-esteem and confidence; and of course reproduction. You'll notice that not once did I mention how often you 'should' be having sex because, ultimately, *quantity* is not what determines satisfaction – it's the *quality* of the experience that matters. Having a realistic understanding of sex in long-term relationships is essential in order to feel satisfied with your sex life. So the question becomes . . . what does 'good enough' look like for you?

What you were taught about sex influences how you think and feel about it. What you were taught drives your attitudes, which then fuels your behaviour. In order to have a great sex life in the long term, not just during the honeymoon phase, we first need to understand our sexual attitudes. Then we need to uncover what lights us up. We need to develop our sexual self-confidence and have realistic expectations so we set ourselves up for satisfaction rather than disappointment.

But how do we actually do this? How do we set ourselves up for satisfaction and great sex? Well, this is exactly what we will be delving into in the following chapters. We are going to explore ways to cultivate intimacy. We will learn about libido and desire and uncover your individual 'brakes' and 'accelerators'. Best of all, we will start to discover how to bring more eroticism into your love life.

Get ready because it's about to get fun!

Summary

- Your sexual history and attitudes are made up of your beliefs, values, expectations and experiences.

- In order to build sexual self-confidence, we need to understand our sexual history and attitudes and how they affect the ways we think about sex, gender and sexuality.

- Sexual shame is a feeling of embarrassment, guilt or self-judgement about the thoughts or feelings you have, the sorts of fantasies you enjoy, the things you desire and the way you engage in sex and sex play.

- Sexual self-confidence, aka sexual self-esteem, is the feeling of being comfortable and capable of engaging in sex and intimacy in a way that pleases you and your partner/s. To build sexual self-confidence we need to focus on getting comfortable in our bodies, challenging unhelpful thoughts, becoming aware of how culture affects our perspective, exploring our likes, dislikes and erotic side, and learning to communicate about sex and be present in our body.

- Lulls in sex, libido and desire are normal. About 45 per cent of relationships will experience some sort of sexual dysfunction at some point in time.

- What is 'good enough' when it comes to sex is determined by you and is different for everyone.

- The goal of sex should not be the outcome, but rather the pleasure, presence and connection you experience.

Activity

Complete your sexual history. Reflect on the following questions and see what comes up for you. The goal is to gain a better understanding of what experiences, beliefs and values have influenced the way you think and feel about sex today.

- Was sex spoken about in your family of origin? If so, how was it discussed?

- How did those early ideas and messages influence how you think about sex now?

- Do you have any cultural or religious beliefs that influence how you think about sex and sexuality?

- What did you learn about sex from your peers growing up?

- What influence did the media have on how you think about sex, desire and sexuality?

- What effect does the media or those early messages have on how you feel about your body?

- What does sex mean to you at this point in your life?

- Which of these formative messages still influence how you engage in sex or your sexuality now?

- When did you first start to have sexual thoughts?

- What was your first sexual experience like?

- How important is sex in your romantic relationships?

- What was your first experience with porn like? Do you remember any thoughts you had about yourself or how sex should be after viewing porn?

- How would you describe the best sex you've ever had? What made it the best?

- Have you had any negative sexual experiences? How has that affected the way you think and feel about sex?

- What beliefs do you have about sex now?

- How comfortable do you feel in your body?

- How comfortable do you feel expressing your sexual desires?

12

Closeness and Intimacy

What type of intimacy helps you feel close and stay connected?

The dictionary defines intimacy as 'something of a personal or private nature'. It speaks of familiarity and closeness.[1] And while the words 'sex' and 'intimacy' have become synonymous in Western culture, when I say intimacy, I am talking not only about sex, but about the broader feeling of being connected and feeling close.

There are many different ways to experience an intimate connection. It comes in many shapes and sizes, however, there are some similarities in how we experience it. We usually feel closeness, connection, and a sense of being seen, heard and understood. We might feel intimate with someone we are dating, a friend, a family member or even a colleague.

Not all types of intimacy will be relevant for all types of relationships but it is helpful to understand the distinctions, because sexual intimacy is often connected to and fuelled by other types of intimacy. This is especially the case with emotional intimacy. When you feel close and connected, it often sparks feelings of desire. One of the ways to relight the fire – and keep it lit – is to focus on the emotional connection.

You needn't be worried about your partner experiencing emotional intimacy with their work colleagues. Experiencing emotional intimacy outside of your primary relationship doesn't mean there is anything wrong. We are relational beings and emotional intimacy is a natural way of feeling close, connected and in tune with others.

Here's a quick rundown of the various types of intimacy you might experience both in and outside of your primary relationship:

- **Emotional intimacy.** Sharing your thoughts, feelings and internal world. This results in you feeling seen, heard and understood. It is also wanting to know and understand your partner/s' internal world and emotional experience which builds trust and embraces vulnerability.
- **Intellectual intimacy.** Having meaningful conversations and connecting over issues you care about. It might involve sharing thoughts and ideas and feeling stimulated by intellectual conversation.
- **Physical intimacy.** Sharing physical closeness and touch. This may be in the form of touching, holding, hugs, kisses and physical closeness.
- **Sexual intimacy.** Engaging in sex and sex play. It could also involve sexual anticipation and flirting.
- **Spiritual intimacy.** Connecting over a shared spiritual belief, value or experience. It might come from feeling a shared purpose or finding meaning in a common goal.

- **Conflict intimacy**. Feeling more connected through resolving issues and disagreements in a productive way.

Invite more intimacy into your relationship

Intimacy is delicate. It's vulnerable. It's like baking; the ingredients are exact and if you forget something, add too much of something or don't follow the instructions . . . you can mess it up. That doesn't mean there is some magic formula to follow because everyone is different, but it does mean we can stuff it up if we don't have the essential ingredients.

To cultivate intimacy, we need the following:

- **Trust**. Being trustworthy and trusting your partner are absolutely essential. Trust is knowing you can rely on that person, and they can rely on you. Trust creates safety, the ability to be vulnerable and is the foundation for all types of intimacy.
- **Vulnerability**. The more vulnerable we are able to be, the more we share about our emotions, feelings, thoughts and the experience of being in our internal world the more connected we feel. The trick is, vulnerability needs to be shared, respected and reciprocated in order to foster intimacy.
- **Communication**. Good, open, honest communication both builds and deepens intimacy as it allows you to share your experience and to truly hear the experience of your partner/s. Being able to communicate well, actively listen and take your partner/s' perspective on board allows you to feel seen, heard, understood and valued.
- **Acceptance**. I believe that acceptance and belonging are what most of us are hoping to find in relationships. There is nothing quite like the feeling of being accepted and loved for who you are. Not having to put on a mask or perform but to simply be

you in all your uniqueness. Fully accepting your partner/s, flaws and all (this does not mean accepting or allowing *all behaviours*) helps them to feel safe and creates a secure connection. When this goes both ways, it is the ultimate ingredient for emotional intimacy.

- **Safety.** To experience intimacy we need emotional safety, intellectual safety, physical safety and sexual safety. Safety is absolutely essential because we need to let our walls down and we cannot and should not do that if it's not safe. We cannot discuss sex and intimacy without also addressing consent. Consent is fundamental and essential. We cannot have safe, intimate connections without it. While I do not get into the topic of consent explicitly in this book, please note that consent is necessary prior to any of the sexual activities we will explore.

- **Touch.** Physical touch, which could be any kind of physical closeness, triggers the release of oxytocin in the brain which is known as the 'love hormone' and increases feelings of empathy, connection and trust. Touch is known to reduce cortisol levels which is the 'stress hormone', lower your heart rate and blood pressure, boost your immune system and improve your mental health.[2]

- **Play.** Enjoying play and fun together is a great way to create and deepen feelings of intimacy. When we play and have fun, we release feel-good hormones in our brain, not only improving our mood and emotional state but helping us feel more connected. We also get a flood of oxytocin, dopamine, serotonin and norepinephrine. These feel-good hormones help us to move into a calm and connected state.

On the other hand, intimacy is damaged by:

- **Breaches of trust.** It's impossible to be truly vulnerable without trust because when we don't have trust we don't feel safe. When we don't feel safe we cannot let our walls down and fully relax and connect. Breaches of trust include being let down, lied to, not keeping agreements or any number of other small hurtful acts. Trust is built and broken in the small moments. It's built through the ways we show up and care for one another, and it's broken in both the things we do and the things we don't do. If your partner has promised to help you with something and they don't, or if you are talking about something important and they are only half paying attention and looking at their phone, it doesn't make you feel close, connected or intimate. It's probably going to make you feel resentful, unimportant and disconnected.
- **Disconnection.** Staying connected in relationships takes conscious time, attention and energy. I have said that sentence many times in this book already but it's true! We start to disconnect when we stop putting in the effort. When we stop prioritising the connection, when we start getting complacent. The more connected you are the more intimacy you are likely to experience. I am not only talking about physical intimacy but other types of intimacy too. While it's normal to have lulls in sex, we don't have to have lulls in connection. In fact, friendship is incredibly important in sustaining our relationships, and should therefore be prioritised.
- **Lack of communication.** Talking to one another, sharing your internal world, feelings, emotions and experiences generates connection and feelings of intimacy. When there is a lack of this type of communication it results in feelings of disconnection. When I say lack of communication, it's not that the

communication is non-existent, it's more that the type of conversation has changed from connecting conversations to life admin or task-focused conversations. Clients often tell me when they have children, the conversations become all about the kids and never about each other. It makes sense that partners feel disconnected. A lack of connecting conversations damages intimacy and so does poor communication and poor conflict management. Learning to communicate effectively and manage conflict builds trust, safety and security, and therefore has a positive effect on generating intimacy.

- **Judgement.** Ah judgement. The thing that ruins everything. Sex . . . ruined, connection . . . ruined, trust . . . ruined, fun . . . ruined, everything . . . ruined! Judging your partner, shaming them or guilting them about who they are, what they want or what they desire will get you nowhere. You know what I'm talking about. That feeling of being judged leading you to shut down, pull away and protect yourself. Leaving you feeling like there is something wrong with you. You feel like a hermit crab retreating into your shell seeking protection and safety. Intimacy requires vulnerability and vulnerability requires safety. *Judgement does not feel safe.* Judgement is also often a statement of superiority in thoughts, beliefs or values and that does not create equality.
- **Lack of safety.** When you don't feel safe emotionally, physically or sexually you are unable to let your walls down and fully connect. You cannot have intimacy without safety.
- **Stagnation.** Getting into a rut leads to intimacy declining. Ruts are a normal part of long-term relationships. We all have them. When we are in a rut we can feel the distance. The key to getting out of a rut is increasing intimate connections. A rut is usually a sign that intimacy and connection have not been

prioritised and have fallen by the wayside, or that one or more of the things that damage it are present.

Create closeness

We create closeness through what we say and do. It's about how you show up for the relationship and your partner/s. It's about how you talk to them, touch them, care for them, and respond to them. We create closeness through our interactions and how we engage.

When you first start dating this might be through texts, calls, spending time together and being very intentional about how and what you share. You go out of your way to show the person you're interested in *why* they should be interested in you. You put your best foot forward and show up as the best version of yourself.

The trouble is, once people become committed they think they don't have to be so intentional anymore and that is where they go wrong. *You need to keep dating.* You need to keep doing the things that made you feel close, connected, wanted and desired. You don't necessarily need to do them as much – I am aware we all have busy lives – but you can't expect to stop doing all the things that got you together and that the same level of closeness will just continue. Deepening intimacy is about reigniting that feeling of being close and connected. Emotionally it's about feeling seen, heard and understood. It's about feeling safe and supported. Sexually, it's about feeling desired, wanted, and free to express yourself without judgement or shame.

To deepen feelings of intimacy with your partner/s you can:

- Tell them what you appreciate about them.
- Express what you like, want and need.
- Tell them what you find attractive about them.

- Make the connection a priority by setting aside time to spend together and being fully present.
- Learn about their likes, dislikes, turn ons and turn offs.
- Increase touch and physical closeness (if that's what they like).
- Give them your full attention when they are talking to you.
- Set aside time regularly for a 'date night' where you can simply focus on one another.
- Turn towards their 'bids for connection'.[3]

The concept of 'bids for connection' comes from John and Julie Gottman. Bids are an attempt to connect or engage in order to establish an emotional connection. In their research, the Gottmans found the more often partners responded to bids for connection, the more satisfied they tended to be in the relationship. On the other hand, partners who had higher rates of missing, turning away from or rejecting their partner/s' bids reported lower relationship satisfaction rates.[4]

Responding to bids for connection helps to create closeness and is the antidote for the pursuer/distancer dynamic. I promised to come back to this and here it is. The pursuer is making a bid for connection by pursuing. They are trying to connect. The distancer by pulling back is rejecting that bid which generally increases feelings of anxiety and insecurity for the pursuer. So, what's the answer . . . for the distancer to turn towards! It doesn't need to be a big one – the distancer may genuinely need space – but the distancer can still turn towards prior to doing so. The benefit will be that it soothes the pursuer making their pursuit less overwhelming. See, it's a win-win!

Maintaining closeness and intimacy requires you to be 'intentional'. You need to be *willing* to make time and space to connect, and to remove any distractions so you can completely focus on your partner/s. It shouldn't feel like a chore but rather an opportunity to continue to learn, to explore more deeply, and to increase feelings of connection. The reward for doing this is a deepening of the emotional bond, an increase of feelings of desire and the creation of a foundation where you are able to better manage the ups and downs of life together.

A final but important note on intimacy. Intimacy requires a balance of giving and receiving. It needs to feel shared, balanced and safe. Consent is an essential part of creating sexual safety. On a basic level, consent is asking if your partner is open and willing to engage physically, emotionally and sexually. True pleasure requires safety; only when we feel free to say no can we truly say yes.

Summary

- Intimacy does not just mean sex. Intimacy is the experience of feeling close and connected.

- There is emotional, intellectual, physical, spiritual, sexual and conflict intimacy.

- The essential ingredients of intimacy are trust, vulnerability, communication, acceptance, safety, touch and play.

- The things that destroy intimacy include breaches of trust, disconnection, lack of communication, judgement, lack of safety and stagnation.

- Intimacy requires closeness. We create closeness through what we say and do. It's about how you show up to the relationship and for your partner/s. It's about how you talk to them, touch them, care for them, and respond to them. We create closeness through how we engage.

Activity

What type of intimacy have you experienced lately? Have a think about the last month and try to identify the types of intimacy you experienced and with whom. How did it feel? What made the experience feel intimate?

- Emotional intimacy: when did you feel close and emotionally connected to someone?

- Intellectual intimacy: when did you have an experience of sharing thoughts and feeling stimulated by intellectual conversation?

- Physical intimacy: when did you have an experience of feeling physically close to someone? It might just have been a really good hug.

- Spiritual intimacy: when did you connect over a shared spiritual belief, value or experience?

- Sexual intimacy: when did you last experience some sexual chemistry, anticipation or flirting?

- Conflict intimacy: when did you last feel close after navigating a conflict?

13

Demystifying Desire

What turns you on?

What does it actually mean to feel desire? It can be difficult to articulate the experience because it's as much physical as it is emotional. It's a yearning, a craving, a wanting and a feeling of being fully consumed. It's being wrapped in thoughts, feelings and fantasies which make you tingle, throb and your heart race. It's like everything else fades away and all you can focus on is them, you, and the present moment.

Desire is that intense feeling of wanting. It's getting swept away by the mere thought of them. It's tasting their lips, smelling their neck and feeling every inch of their body. It's their pleasure being just as important as your own. It's feeling your body respond to them. It's their sounds, their movements, their touch. It's exciting, it's primal and it's liberating.

Embracing and experiencing our desires gives us a level of freedom from the caged world in which we live our day-to-day lives. Through our desires we can connect with our most vulnerable, uncensored selves. When we share that with a partner, that's when we experience true sexual intimacy.

While it's easy to get lost in feelings of desire in the beginning of a relationship, the more familiar we become with one another, and the more we merge our lives, the harder it can become to experience sexual ecstasy. It gets harder because of the pressure, the expectation, the obligation and because there's less newness, less excitement and more familiarity. People think they *should* want sex, and often feel like there is something wrong with them when they don't. I want to take a moment here to say there is *nothing* wrong with you if you're not that interested in sex. It might be that sex just isn't that important to you, or it might be more to do with the type and quality of sex you're having. Whatever it is, you are normal and 100 per cent not alone.

The most common thing that brings people to sex therapy is mismatched libidos, which means they want different amounts of sex, but there is no research that says the amount of sex you have has any influence on how good it is or how satisfied you will be. It's about quality, not quantity, after all.

So, what *is* important? How do you have 'quality sex'? This chapter is all about helping you understand your own desire, acquainting yourself with your partner/s' desire and giving you simple tools to create a sex life that you love. To do this, let's begin by differentiating between desire and arousal.

Sexual desire refers to your interest in sex and sex play. It's more about the mental, emotional and psychological experience. Sexual arousal refers to your physical responses to desire. Arousal is the way your body responds when you experience desire. Your heart rate might increase, your genitals might throb, you might sweat, you might get wet or hard.

In a perfect world, when you feel desire your body also becomes aroused, however this is often not the case. Sometimes, you might have all the feels but for whatever reason, your body does not respond how you want it to. This is called 'arousal non-accordance'. It can be confusing, because your partner might think you're not into it, or you might think there is something wrong when in actual fact, arousal non-accordance is quite common. In order to better understand your arousal, you first need to explore your desire.

We are all different and therefore we all experience desire differently. That said, it tends to be ignited by certain things, such as:

- **Your senses.** This might be the smell of a nice perfume on your partner/s' neck, or creating a beautiful space where you can be intimate or being touched in a certain place or way. It could also relate to something you see, hear or taste.
- **Your mind.** It might be created by fantasies, sexy thoughts, memories or any kind of anticipation. It's the thinking about what is going to happen and the imagining that fuels the desire.
- **The exploration.** For some people it's about pushing the limits and trying new things. For these people desire is connected with the newness, the excitement and the exploration.

Desire is deeply personal and you might relate to one or all of these elements. You might feel desire out of the blue, in response to some stimulus, or it may depend entirely on the context.

In *Come As You Are*, the American sex educator and researcher Dr Emily Nagoski explains three key types of desire:[1]

- 'Spontaneous desire' is when you feel sexual desire without any external stimulus. You might randomly get turned on and want sex, which usually means you're the one initiating.

- 'Responsive desire' is when you feel sexual desire in response to some sort of stimulus. This means in order to get turned on you'll have to experience something that triggers desire. This might mean you will rarely be the one initiating but you usually get into it when your partner initiates.
- 'Contextual desire' is when feeling desire is highly dependent on the environment and situation. You might be quite sensitive to the world around you and need things to be a particular way in order for desire to emerge.

It's helpful to know the way you experience desire because it will likely affect your sexual experiences in your relationship. Imagine you have two responsive people . . . who is going to be the one to initiate? Or what happens if there is one spontaneous and one contextual . . . the spontaneous person is probably going to feel like they always initiate and that things have to be 'just so' in order for the contextual person to respond.

It doesn't stop there. We also have what are known as 'libido brakes and accelerators'.[2] This concept also comes from Dr Nagoski and describes the 'Dual Control Model' which explores how we all have things that increase our feelings of desire and arousal, and things that diminish it.[3] As the name suggests, brakes slow you down and turn you off. Some people's brakes will be incredibly touchy while others' will be relatively loose. Accelerators on the other hand are anything that gets you going and drives your sexual desire. They intensify your feelings. So, what are some common brakes and accelerators?

Examples of brakes include:

- Smells such as body odour, bad breath, or not being in a clean environment.
- Feeling rushed, stressed or overwhelmed.

- Not liking your partner very much due to unresolved issues in the relationship.
- Not feeling desired by your partner or feeling self-conscious.
- The environment e.g. the house being messy and dirty dishes filling up the sink.

Examples of accelerators include:

- Feeling wanted and desired by your partner.
- Being in a clean and tidy space where there are pleasant smells, flattering lighting and clean sheets.
- Feeling safe with and connected to your partner.
- Having plenty of time.
- Not being overly stressed or overwhelmed by other areas of your life.

For some people, doing the dishes is foreplay! If you're someone who is really affected by the state of your environment, then having a partner who anticipates this and does things to help you get in the mood, like making sure the dishes are done and the sink is clean, can be the same or even better than physical foreplay.

Desire and arousal are not just about touching one another. They are as much about the anticipation and the environment as anything else. So, learning about your partner/s' brakes and accelerators can be an incredibly helpful way to focus your attention on the things that work, not the things that don't.

Even when we know all the tips and tricks, sometimes we still miss the mark. This is because mismatched desire levels are very common. Often, people want different amounts of sex which creates a 'desire gap'. This gap can be due to health, stress, life circumstances, relationship factors or simply preference. It could also be that you seek sex for different reasons e.g. some people want sex when they're stressed to help them cope; others find stress a total desire destroyer! Some people want sex to feel connected whereas others need to feel connected to want sex. Navigating the desire gap is more about understanding than it is about fixing, so exploring your desire and creating realistic expectations is the place to start. Start by asking yourself:

- Do you have any beliefs about how often people in relationships should have sex? Where do those beliefs come from? How do they make you feel?
- When do you tend to feel desire? Is there a certain time of day, location or context?
- What does partnered sex mean to you? What do you get from sex with a partner that you don't get from solo sex?
- What is the best sexual experience you've had with your partner? Or with a past partner if single? What made it so good?
- What makes a sexual experience satisfying? Is it the emotional connection? It is an orgasm or ejaculation?
- Do you talk about sex and communicate your desires?
- How do you navigate the moments when you're not in the mood and have to turn down your partner/s?

Some people want sex to feel connected whereas others need to feel connected to want sex.

Once you've asked yourself these questions, ask your partner/s. So many of the sexual challenges we face actually come from not communicating. We keep things to ourselves and they become big issues. We obsess, we worry, we create shame when all the while our partner/s are thinking and feeling the exact same way. There is nothing to be ashamed of when it comes to sex, desire, libido and confidence levels. Society has made sex taboo but if we talked about it more we would realise just how normal our collective experiences truly are.

Society has made sex taboo but if we talked about it more we would realise just how normal our collective experiences truly are.

For anyone in a long-term relationship who would like to know what really matters when it comes to re-establishing desire, this is what I have found. The things that matter are curiosity, exploration, the friendship, and actually prioritising the sexual connection. It's not glamorous . . . but hey, it sure is simple and attainable! So, what do each of these look like?

- **Curiosity.** Being curious about your partner and open to exploring is essential. We can't just assume we know what they like, or even if we do know, that what they like won't change. People are complex and ever-evolving so what we liked a year ago, a week ago, hell even a day ago can change. Get curious and explore. Sexual exploration and curiosity create a space where you can feel free to express your full sexual self. It creates a space free of judgement where you can figure out what works for you. Staying curious might involve talking about sex, role playing, exploring fantasies, trying new toys or positions or whatever play and exploration looks like for you. The idea is that you continually create a space where you can be open to learning about each other's bodies, likes, turn ons, fantasies and desires.

- **Friendship.** It's no secret that the friendship is incredibly import-ant in a relationship. I mean, I did dedicate a whole chapter to it so I'm sure it won't come as a surprise! The friendship also affects the kind of sex you have and how you feel about sex with your partner/s. If you're annoyed with one another, full of resentment for the ways they have let you down recently and are not feeling connected, then that will more than likely be reflected in the sex. I'm not saying the sex won't be decent, but it probably won't be great. It will likely be 'maintenance sex' rather than intimate and exciting sex (maintenance sex is where it's used to maintain the relationship). If you want to have great sex you need to take care of your relationship. You need to make your partner/s feel wanted, desired and appreciated. If you're in a good place relationship-wise, you're far more likely to have great sex. Another element which really helps is to increase non-sexual touching. This means hugging more (especially after sex), kissing more and being conscious of the different ways you can be physically intimate that are not sexual.
- **Prioritising it.** If sex is important to you, then you need to prioritise it. It's really that simple. When you make it a priority you make time for it. When you make it a priority, you are saying, 'This is important to me'. Prioritising it might mean arranging regular date nights, doing things that make you feel connected, or simply making time and space for one another. It could even be bringing back a bit of flirting and anticipation just for fun!

By staying curious, focusing on the friendship and making sex a priority you can keep the fire lit. It won't necessarily burn as bright and hot as when you first started dating – the reality is sex changes over time – but that doesn't mean it needs to die out. Many people actually find the more they feel comfortable and know their partner/s' bodies the hotter and sexier the sex gets over time.

Want to be one of those people? To do that requires you to embrace your erotic self. Through eroticism we can explore our urges, desires, thoughts and dreams. We can build anticipation and tension. This is exactly what we are going to focus on next: connecting to your erotic self.

Summary

- Sexual desire refers to your interest in sex and sex play. It's about the mental, emotional and psychological experience.

- Sexual arousal refers to your physical responses to desire. Arousal is the way your body responds when you experience desire.

- Desire tends to be ignited by different elements including your senses, your mind and exploration.

- There are three different types of desire: spontaneous, contextual and responsive.

- We all have libido 'brakes' and 'accelerators'. These are things that increase our feelings of desire and arousal, and things that diminish it.

- The things that truly matter when it comes to re-establishing desire are curiosity and exploration, the friendship and prioritising the sexual connection.

Activity

Have a think about the following questions. If you have a partner/s I recommend asking one another these questions.

- How would you describe desire?

- What does it feel like in your body?

- What ignites desire for you?

- What are your brakes and accelerators?

- What type of libido resonates with you: spontaneous, responsive or contextual?

- What are your sexual boundaries? What feels okay and not okay for you sexually?

And if you are in a relationship:

- How could you be more curious and explorative?

- How could you deepen the friendship?

- What could you do to prioritise the sexual connection?

14

Embracing the Erotic

Explore and embrace your erotic self

Eros was the Greek god of love, sex and desire. According to Greek mythology, he was thought to have been the son of Aphrodite – the goddess of love, lust, fertility, passion and pleasure. Aphrodite was said to have been far more important than Eros in the grand scheme of things, however, for various reasons Eros left a bigger mark on our language.

The word 'erotic' is derived from the Greek word *eros* and means to 'arouse sexual love or desire'.[1] Eros speaks of a type of passionate, pleasure-focused, fun, sexual love. Eroticism, which is the act of being erotic, isn't just about the act of sex, it's about the experience of passion, lust and pleasure. Eroticism is found in the waiting and wanting. It is the exploration of our inner urges, desires, thoughts and dreams. It's the anticipation and tension that builds in our minds and bodies.

It's not hard for people to have decent sex. Most people are pretty satisfied with decent sex but I don't want you to have just decent sex. I want you to have erotic, passionate, connected and pleasure-focused sex! To do this, you need to explore and embrace your erotic self.

This chapter explores how to connect with your erotic self and how you can bring more eroticism into your love and sex life. The goal is to help you to better understand your sexual self, to build confidence, to allow you to explore your desires and, hopefully, encourage you to go on this adventure with your current or future partner/s.

Let's begin with a little self-reflection.

Uncover

In the last few chapters we've talked about your sexual history. Now we are going to uncover who you are as an erotic being. Embracing your erotic self requires you to give yourself permission to be an erotic and sexual being. It's about embracing the messiness and the awkwardness, and learning about yourself and your preferences. To do this, we start by exploring our innermost selves. The selves most of us hide away because of the sexual taboos in society. The selves that when brought out into the light and embraced can bring great pleasure. It's time to get comfortable and reflect upon the following questions:

- What do you want from sex?
- What are your fantasies? If you could imagine a scenario where you were completely swept away by passion and desire, how would it look?
- What's your favourite sex scene from a movie?
- What are your innermost desires?
- What brings you pleasure? E.g. closeness, kissing, penetration, rubbing.

- How does your body respond to different stimuli? E.g. touch, pressure, temperature.
- How do you feel about your body? Does how you feel get in the way of expressing yourself sexually?
- Do you feel like you can explore your sexuality free from judgement? Do you find yourself being judgemental?
- Do you have any expectations about yourself sexually or of your partner/s that may not be realistic?
- Do you have friends or other people you can openly and honestly talk about sex with?
- How is your sexual communication with your partner/s?

It may not sound sexy, but embracing and exploring the erotic starts with answering these foundational questions. It starts with getting comfortable in yourself, learning to talk about sex and being open and willing to explore.

Connect – self and lover

Now it's time to connect. Presence and connection with the self are incredibly important. I often hear about how people cannot remain present and connected to themselves long enough to orgasm. They might be able to orgasm just fine when they are by themselves, but when they're with their partner/s they struggle to relax and sufficiently connect to truly experience pleasure. A big part of pleasure is being connected to our bodies, being present and being able to connect with our partner/s.

Start with you. Start by connecting with yourself and learning what you like. Take some time to explore your body, to touch yourself and see what feels good. Notice if you get into your head and if you do, notice what helps bring you back to the present moment. Think about what you need in order to feel safe. If we are to be fully present and connected we need to feel safe. Some people have the luxury of feeling safe and being able to connect with their bodies when they have casual sex, but for others it's quite the opposite. What helps you to feel safe in your body?

A tantra exercise I like, which always helps me to get present, is something called 'eye gazing'. If I am alone and wanting to feel connected to myself I will sit in front of a mirror cross-legged with one hand on my heart and one hand on my stomach. I then simply focus on looking at myself in the eyes and taking long deep breaths for three minutes. This practice helps me tune in and connect with myself and my body. If you would like to try this with your partner/s, simply sit facing each other and look into one another's eyes. See how it feels to hold one another's gaze and breathe in sync.

First you connect with yourself, then you can connect with your lover. When I say 'connect' I am talking about creating a space where you can be open with one another, where you can take your time to get to know one another's bodies and explore each other's desires.

I will get into this a bit more in a moment but for now, what I want you to know is no-one is born with a sexual manual. Being a great lover is learned. It's learned by connecting, exploring and embracing. Everyone's body is different so the thing your ex loved will not be the same thing as your current or future partner/s. Getting to know their bodies, their turn ons and what makes them feel comfortable takes time.

Being a great lover is learned. It's learned by connecting, exploring and embracing.

One of the main reasons people struggle to have great, connected sex is because they aren't talking about it. So, talk about what you like, explore one another and take your time. Connecting erotically isn't about just getting to orgasm so take that goal off the table and just focus on connection.

Environment

Your environment has a significant effect on how you feel. I don't know about you, but there is no way in hell I am able to get in the mood when my home is a complete mess and the sheets aren't clean. It might sound fickle to some, but your environment can affect your mood, stress levels and ability to connect with your body and experience pleasure.

Ask yourself when do you feel most relaxed? Where do you feel most excited? It might be in a certain room of the house. Or it might be in the car, or the bath, or in the backyard under the stars. If you think about where and when you get turned on, are there any environmental themes at play? Is it when you're on holiday because you don't have to worry about work or the chores that need doing around the house? Is it first thing in the morning when you're half asleep?

Spend some time thinking about what the perfect environment would be to help you connect with yourself and embrace a passionate connection with your partner/s.

Imagination

One of the biggest dampeners on people's sex lives is getting stuck in a routine. When I say routine, I mean initiating sex in the same way, at the same time, and having the same sex in the same positions. Sure, that's decent sex and does the trick if you just want to orgasm or ejaculate, but that's all it does. This is why people often stop wanting sex. The quality of the sex they're having just isn't worth wanting.

If you want to have connected, passionate and erotic sex, then you need to be willing to use your imagination. Our imagination is one of our most important and valuable tools, not least when it comes to desire. Our imagination helps us to explore in our minds what people might feel like, taste like or smell like, and how we might experience an intimate moment with them. Using your imagination gets you aroused before anything has even happened. It triggers your body to anticipate a touch so that when the touch becomes reality, the feeling is delightfully intensified.

Using your imagination to embrace desires fuels excitement. It also gives you ideas of how to spice things up. Using your imagination might mean thinking of different ways you can touch one another, different roles you can play, or different props or toys you can use. Your imagination is limitless. Let it roll and see where it takes you.

Play

Sex doesn't need to be so serious. We tend to think it is which can make it super stressful at times but really, sex can just be about play and enjoyment. There is so much pressure put on sex that it's no wonder people have so many issues with it. It's one of the most taboo, least talked about areas of relationships and yet it's something many people (though not all) engage in. Sex is about pleasure, it's about feeling good and enjoying the present moment with your partner/s. It's about connecting and being intimate. It shouldn't be overly strategic or planned (unless you like that type of thing) and it shouldn't be something you feel like you 'have' to do to keep your partner/s happy.

People often tell me they have a low libido. But when I dig a little deeper, what they really have a problem with is the *quality* of their sex. It may be that it's monotonous or not very exciting and they don't feel connected to their partner/s. As I say, sex should be fun! Not another chore.

Focus on sexual or erotic play. Really prioritise the sexual play, erotically caress each other and build the tension. Allow yourself to laugh at awkward sounds, the messiness and the humanness of sex. It's not perfect, it's real and the more you can play and have fun with it, the more relaxed you will feel and the more pleasure you will experience.

Pleasure

I've said it before and I will say it again, the focus should be on pleasure, not on the outcome. Eroticism is alllll about pleasure. It's about the sensual experience, the passion, the drive, the desire and the yearning. It's about the psychosexual experience, not just the end game. Sure, the outcome is great but is it as good as having a deeply erotic sexual experience? Personally, I would say no, it's not.

When you have a deeply erotic sexual experience it can be totally consuming. Your mind, your body – everything – is wrapped up in the moment, utterly absorbed in every sound, movement, taste and touch. Focusing on pleasure allows you to slow things down and also helps if you struggle with low sexual self-confidence. Ask your partner/s to show you what pleasures them, and show them what pleasures you. Give yourself space, with no time restrictions to just explore what feels good and creates pleasure without focusing on orgasm or ejaculation. In fact, you might even agree to build the tension and bring one another to the point of orgasm, without going over the edge. Focus on how it feels in your body, the electricity and the energy. If your only goal is pleasure, it takes a lot of pressure off the experience.

Exploration

Sexual exploration is a process. We are always changing, learning and growing, and what we desire and enjoy today may be different to what we like tomorrow. We need to continue to explore our sexual selves, and our partner/s'. Sexual exploration refers to the ongoing discovery of your body, your pleasures, your fantasies and your desires. Sexual exploration helps you to learn about your body, *what* you're into and *who* you're into. Sexual exploration might involve enhancing the experience of pleasure or investigating your sexuality.

Sexual exploration is associated with increased sexual self-confidence and 'self-concept' – the way you see yourself. It helps us to feel more secure in ourselves, to know ourselves more deeply and to connect with our partner/s. Knowing yourself and being open to exploration also creates a secure space where your partner/s can feel free to do the same. It creates an open, non-judgemental environment that facilitates play and pleasure. Really, there are no downsides to sexual exploration. It helps you to better understand yourself, your pleasure and your partner/s' pleasure. You really can't go wrong – it's another win-win.

Embracing your erotic self might sound like it's a psychological process rather than a physical one and in all honesty, that's because it is. Your most important sex organ is your brain! The way you think and feel about sex as well as how you see yourself as a sexual being greatly influence how comfortable you feel engaging in sex and sex play.

It affects the level of pleasure you're able to experience and how present and comfortable you are. The goal is not to have erotic, passionate, desire-filled sex every time but rather to be able to deeply connect to yourself and your body so you can be more *pleasure*-focused and less *outcome*-focused. Having great sex isn't

214

about how long it lasts or whether or not you orgasm, it's about the lead up, the anticipation, the presence, the connection, the touch, the desire, the electricity and the pleasure.

Think pleasure first. Always, pleasure first.

Summary

- The word erotic which is derived from the Greek work Eros (inspired by the god of love) means to 'arouse sexual love or desire'.[2] Eros speaks of a type of passionate, pleasure-focused, fun, sexual love.

- Eroticism isn't just about the act of sex, it's about the experience of passion, lust and pleasure. Eroticism is the exploration of our inner urges, desires, thoughts and dreams. It's the anticipation and tension that builds in our minds and bodies.

- The process of connecting with your erotic self is as follows:
  - Uncover: uncover your innermost wants and desires. What feels good?
  - Connection: practise connecting to yourself and your partner/s. This involves practising being present in your body.
  - Environment: become aware of the effect of your environment and what you need to be able to embrace desire and passion.
  - Imagination: if you want to have connected, passionate and erotic sex, then you need to be willing to use your imagination.
  - Play: sex isn't that serious. We tend to think it is which makes it super stressful at times but really, sex can be about play and enjoyment.
  - Pleasure: focus on pleasure, not on the outcome.
  - Exploration: we are always changing, learning and growing and what we desire and enjoy today may be different to what we like tomorrow. We need to continue to explore our sexual selves, and our partner/s'.

Activity

Let your imagination run wild. Lie down on your bed or your couch and get comfortable. Dim the lights and even light a nice candle. Now, I want you to take ten minutes to delve into a sexual fantasy. Simply allow your mind to wander. Use the prompts below if needed.

- Where are you? What is the scenario?

- Can you smell anything, see anything, taste anything?

- Do you notice any feelings in your body? How would you describe them?

- Is anyone there with you? If so, what are they doing?

- What are you wanting? Where do you feel that wanting in your body?

- How would it feel to get what you want?

- Imagine it plays out, getting what you want; how can you slow down and savour that experience?

- Simply notice the feelings in your body, the desires and the fantasies, and allow your mind to continue along the journey as long as it feels good.

- Once you are done, ask yourself: what was it about that fantasy that felt so good? Think in terms of environment, play, pleasure, exploration and connection.

Bringing It All Together

So, the question is, are you willing?

We're near the end of our journey. The big question is: are you willing to show up and do what it takes to create a relationship that heals, nourishes and yet also challenges and helps you to grow? The purpose of relationships is not for them to be easy; the purpose of relationships is to help us grow, connect and become the best version of ourselves. In order do that, relationships need to act as mirrors.

Relationships will bring up all the things we are trying to avoid. Relationships force us to address them. This can be uncomfortable, but it doesn't mean it needs to be difficult. The more we resist the things which come to the surface, the more we try to suppress them, the more challenging they become. We don't need to fight, we can surrender, we can welcome, we can move into ease and allow ourselves to grow, change and embrace the new.

You have the choice and the power to create the connections you want, you just need to be *willing*. Of course, you also need to choose partner/s who are also willing and ready to engage in that process because you cannot do it alone. There needs to be mutual commitment and even then, unfortunately, nothing is guaranteed.

Sometimes we can go all in, we can try everything within our powers and there is still something missing. Sometimes, no matter what we do, we just can't get that intimate love back, we can't get over the past hurts. Sometimes, sadly, it's quite simply too far gone.

The sad truth is, some relationships are meant to end.

I know this all too well. I too have grieved deep heartbreak. I have grieved the loss of love that I thought would last, love that I truly wanted with every inch of my body to save, but couldn't. I am familiar with the feeling of being all in and having to admit to myself that they are not. Sometimes they are giving everything they can, but the sad truth is your 'all in' and their 'all in' may be too far apart.

Sometimes that is the harsh reality; people are just not where you are, they may not have the capacity or the emotional availability to truly go all in with you. That puts you in a position where you must decide whether you stay and accept the level of love they have capacity for and how they are able to show up, or you send them love and set them free. In the end, it's not your job to change them, fix them, or push them to be someone else. It's your job to show up, go all in and determine whether they are able to meet you in a place that will allow you to grow and develop . . . together.

Being in a relationship is a choice. It's a choice you make each and every day in the way you show up, how you communicate and what you choose to invest. The truth is, the type of relationship I write about in this book is not an investment everyone will be ready, willing or able to make. This type of relationship requires a level of emotional maturity and availability that isn't experienced by everyone.

It's not to say everyone *can't* experience it, of course they can, but it requires a degree of commitment to self-awareness and personal growth that for some, may not be a priority. Others may simply not have the capacity. If self-awareness and personal growth are not important to them, if they want a low-effort and low-maintenance relationship, that's their choice. We must not judge them for that. All we can do is choose whether or not we wish to be in that relationship with them.

What we put in, we get out, so if you want a secure, connected and healthy relationship that helps you to thrive and become the best version of yourself, then you need to choose people who are also willing to invest in that process. Equally and wholeheartedly.

No-one is expecting you to find or be the perfect partner. I am a realist and am not interested in creating unattainable expectations. To me progress is the goal, not perfection.

There are going to be times on the journey ahead when your attachment wounds pop up and become activated. That's natural. There will be times when you realise the beliefs you have about relationships may not actually be realistic. That's normal too. You might become aware of some unproductive coping strategies you need to address and work on within yourself, or you might notice your emotions are starting to negatively affect your partner/s and the relationship so you need to learn how to regulate them. It's nothing to be ashamed of and doesn't mean you're not making progress.

The goal is not and never has been perfection. There is no such thing as perfection when it comes to relationships with yourself or with others because we are always changing and we are always learning. The goal is progress. The goal is to notice the things that aren't working and respond with enough openness and compassion to see it as an opportunity for growth. The goal is to understand your wounds, and to work on healing them. And it's about discovering your partner/s' wounds so you can be sensitive to them too.

We all have wounds, we all have a past and we all have issues we are working through. A colleague once shared an analogy from Bowen therapy which really resonated with me. It goes like this: imagine you have a bruise on your arm. It's underneath your sleeve so people don't know it's there but it's very tender when people accidentally brush up against it. This bruise represents your past hurts, sensitivities, wounds, triggers and pain. When you meet someone new and they accidentally brush up against your bruise and cause you pain, if they apologise and are sincere, you can easily forgive them because they were unaware. If, however, they keep 'accidentally' brushing up against it as time goes on, even though they know it's there, you'll slowly build resentment because they are not being cautious or considerate of your history and pain.

We all have bruises, and while it is our individual responsibility to understand them, work on healing them and not let them fester, it is also a partner/s' responsibility to be gentle and considerate. We need to be mindful of one another's bruises. We need to be thoughtful with our words and sensitive with our actions. Doing this demonstrates care, love, respect and awareness.

This stuff isn't easy but it is relatively simple which means if you just keep at it, you will notice improvements. If you just keep working on the communication in your relationship, even if at times you stuff up, you will notice improvements. If you keep checking in after a conflict and exploring how you could have navigated it better with compassion and empathy, you will notice improvements. If you become more considerate of your partner/s, think about their needs, become a better listener and prioritise the relationship, the connection will deepen, and if you talk openly about sex and get comfy exploring your erotic side, your sex life will become more delicious. It's about taking small and consistent steps in the direction of your goal. If your goal is a nourishing, connected, safe and intimate relationship, then you are on your way.

I hope that this book helps you to know that you deserve a love who shows up, who puts in the effort and who is willing to create secure foundations with you. I hope it reminds you that wanting an equal partnership is not too much to ask. It may not be fifty/fifty all the time, but it needs to feel balanced. I hope that this book reminds you that really great relationships aren't found, they're built. It's not about finding the perfect partner, it's about choosing someone you care about who is ready and willing to engage in that process of co-creation with you.

After all, love is not the only thing you need. Love does not sustain relationships indefinitely. Sure, we need it, but love alone will not keep you safe, make you feel supported and help you grow into the best version of yourself.

May this book help you discern whom to give your heart to and allow you to experience all the healing that comes with safe love. May it help you to know and be able to articulate when they are not all in with you and to know when it's time to walk away. May this book help you reconnect and feel closer to your partner/s so you can experience the joy of intimacy once more. May this book give you what you need to heal from past hurts, set your intentions for your relationship future, and guide your actions on the road ahead. And may it help you open up your heart to give and receive deep, safe and intimate love.

Acknowledgements

Thank you to all of the incredible people who helped bring this book to life. Thank you for giving me the opportunity to use all I have learned from my relationships, from the pain, the grief, the love, the joy, the growth, the healing and allowing me to repurpose it in the hope that it will help others grow and heal too.

Thank you to the team at Penguin Random House and Ashwin Khurana for trusting me and helping make this dream come true.

Thank you to Rod Morrison, my brilliant editor, who was incredibly patient with me as I went back and forth over these pages more times than I can count.

Thank you to my fellow therapists and friends who provided me with such valuable guidance, support and encouragement while writing this book . . . Carly, Judy and Mel.

Thank you to my amazing family, friends and partner for supporting me, loving me and fully accepting me.

Thank you to those of you who like, share, comment and engage with my posts on social media and provide me with such vulnerable insight into your lives. Your messages bring a smile to my face every single day.

And thank you, dear reader, for picking up this book. I hope that by reading it you will find ways to connect more deeply, love more intimately and create a bond that feels safe and nourishing, and that encourages you to become the best version of yourself.

Sending love,

Lucille

Resources

On dating

Guenther, Jeff and Happ, Kate, *Big Dating Energy*, Voracious, New York, 2024.
Tatkin, Stan, *Wired for Dating*, New Harbinger Publications, Oakland, 2016.
Ury, Logan, *How To Not Die Alone*, Simon & Schuster, New York, 2022.

On relationships

Carnes, Patrick J, *The Betrayal Bond*, HCI, Boca Raton, 2015.
Fern, Jessica, *Polysecure*, Scribe Publications, Victoria, 2022.
——, *Polywise*, Thornapple Press, Victoria, 2023.
Gottman, John and DeClaire, Joan, *The Relationship Cure*, Three Rivers Press, New York, 2001.
Gottman, John and Silver, Nan, *The Seven Principles for Making Marriage Work*, Orion, New York, 2023.
——, *What Makes Love Last*, Simon & Schuster, New York, 2013.
Gottman, John et al., *Eight Dates*, Workman Publishing, New York, 2019.
Hendrix, Harville and Lakelly Hunt, Helen, *Getting the Love You Want*, St Martins Griffin, New York, 2019.
Hill, Jess, *See What You Made Me Do*, Black Inc, Melbourne, 2019.
Jansen, David and Newman, Margaret, *Really Relating*, Random House, Sydney, 1998.
Kirshenbaum, Mira, *Too Good to Leave, Too Bad to Stay*, Plume, New York, 1997.
Perel, Esther, *Mating in Captivity*, Hodder & Stoughton, London, 2007.
——, *The State of Affairs*, Hodder & Stoughton, London, 2019.
Real, Terry, *Fierce Intimacy*, Sounds True Adult, Louisville, 2018.
Tatkin, Stan, *We Do*, Sounds True Adult, Louisville, 2018.
——, *Wired for Dating*, New Harbinger Publications, Oakland, 2016.
——, *Your Brain on Love*, Sounds True Adult, Louisville, 2013.

On sex

Grace, Georgia, *The Modern Guide to Sex*, HarperCollins, 2024.
Marin, Vanessa and Marin, Xander, *Sex Talks*, Simon Element, New York, 2023.
Morse, Emily, *Smart Sex*, Park Row, New York, 2023.
Nagoski, Emily, *Come As You Are*, Simon & Schuster, New York, 2015.
——, *Come Together*, Random House, New York, 2024.
Otten, Chantelle, *The Sex Ed You Never Had*, Allen & Unwin, Sydney, 2021.
Tanner, Casey, *Feel It All*, Harper, New York, 2024.

On your relationship with yourself

Brown, Brené, *Braving the Wilderness*, Random House, New York, 2017.
——, *Dare to Lead*, Ebury, New York, 2018.
——, *Daring Greatly*, Avery, New York, 2012.
——, *The Gifts of Imperfection*, Hazelden, Center City, 2010.
——, *The Power of Vulnerability*, Sounds True Adult, Louisville, 2013.
——, *Rising Strong*, Random House, New York, 2015.
Brown, Brené and Burke, Tarana, *You Are Your Best Thing*, Random House, New York, 2021.
Doyle, Glennon, *Untamed*, Dial Press, New York, 2020.
Fernandez-Preiksa, Alexis, *The Neuroscience of Self-Love*, Affirm, Melbourne, 2022.

On mindset

Dispenza, Joe, *Breaking the Habit of Being Yourself*, Hay House, Carlsbad, 2012.
Ellis, Albert, *How to Stubbornly Refuse to Make Yourself Miserable About Anything, Yes Anything*, Lyle Stuart, Secaucus, 1988.
Tawwab, Nedra Glover, *Set Boundaries, Find Peace*, TarcherPerigee, New York, 2021.

On attachment and your relationship with your caregivers

Burke Harris, Nadine, *The Deepest Well*, Mariner Books, New York, 2018.
Gibson, Lindsay C, *Adult Children of Emotionally Immature Parents*, New Harbinger Publications, Oakland, 2015.
Levine, Amir and Heller, Rachel SF, *Attached*, TarcherPerigee, New York, 2010.
Pharaon, Vienna, *The Origins of You*, G. P. Putnam's Sons, New York, 2023.
Poole Heller, Diane, *Healing Your Attachment Wounds*, Sounds True Adult, Louisville, 2017.
Webb, Jonice, *Running on Empty*, Morgan James Publishing, New York, 2012.

Support services

Australia – 1800 RESPECT. Call 1800 737 732 or visit
https://www.1800respect.org.au/
US and Canada – The Hotline. Call 1800 799 7233 or visit https://www.thehotline.org/
UK – Refuge UK. Call 0808 2000 247 or visit https://www.nationaldahelpline.org.uk/
List of international women and children helplines
https://wave-network.org/list-of-helplines-in-46-countries/

Endnotes

Chapter 1 Beliefs

1   'Conditioning', *APA Dictionary of Psychology*, American Psychological Association, Washington, 2024.
2   Hurrelmann K and Bauer U, *Socialisation During the Life Course*, Routledge, Philadelphia, 2018.
3   Pohl RF (Ed.), *Cognitive Illusions*, Routledge, Philadelphia, 2022.
4   Bowlby J, *A Secure Base*, Routledge, Philadelphia, 2012.
5   Butler J, *Gender Trouble*, Routledge, Philadelphia, 1999.
6   Sagiv L and Schwartz SH, 'Personal Values Across Cultures', *Annual Review of Psychology*, 73, 2022, pp. 517–46.

Chapter 2 Drivers

1   Bowlby J, *Attachment and Loss*, Random House, London, 1969.
2   Salter Ainsworth MD and Bell SM, 'Attachment, exploration, and separation: Illustrated by the behavior of one-year-olds in a strange situation', *The Life Cycle: Readings in Human Development*, Columbia University Press, 1981, pp. 57–71.
3   Ainsworth MD, 'Patterns of attachment behavior shown by the infant in interaction with his mother', *Merrill-Palmer Quarterly of Behavior and Development*, 10(1), 1964, pp. 51–8.
4   Mickelson KD, Kessler RC and Shaver PR, 'Adult attachment in a nationally representative sample', *Journal of Personality and Social Psychology*, 73(5), 1997, pp. 1092–1106.

5   Keller H, 'Universality claim of attachment theory: Children's socioemotional development across cultures', *Proceedings of the National Academy of Sciences*, 6;115(45), 2018, pp. 11414–9.
6   Furrow JL et al., *The Emotionally Focused Casebook*, Routledge, Philadelphia, 2011.
7   Furrow JL et al., *The Emotionally Focused Casebook*, Routledge, Philadelphia, 2011.
8   Stayton DJ et al., 'Development of separation behavior in the first year of life: Protest, following, and greeting', *Developmental Psychology*, 9(2), 1973, p. 213.

Chapter 3 Safe Love

1   Salter Ainsworth MD and Bell SM, 'Attachment, exploration, and separation: Illustrated by the behavior of one-year-olds in a strange situation', *The Life Cycle: Readings in Human Development*, Columbia University Press, 1981, pp. 57–71.
2   Ainsworth MD, 'Patterns of attachment behavior shown by the infant in interaction with his mother', *Merrill-Palmer Quarterly of Behavior and Development*, 10(1), 1964, pp. 51–8.
3   Schwartz RC and Sweezy M, *Internal Family Systems Therapy*, Guilford Publications, New York, 2019.
4   Johnson S, *Hold Me Tight*, Hachette, London, 2011.
5   'Gaslighting', *Merriam Webster Dictionary*, Springfield, 2024.
6   New South Wales Government, 'What are the impacts of coercive control?', Department of Communities and Justice, 2024.

Chapter 4 Emotions

1   Gottman JM et al., 'Parental meta-emotion philosophy and the emotional life of families: theoretical models and preliminary data', *Journal of Family Psychology*, 10(3), 1996, p. 243.
2   Randall AK and Bodenmann G, 'The role of stress on close relationships and marital satisfaction', *Clinical Psychology Review*, 29(2), 2009, pp. 105–15.
3   Beck JS, *Cognitive Behavior Therapy*, Guilford Publications, New York, 2021.
4   Linehan M, *DBT Skills Training Manual*, Guilford Publications, New York, 2014.
5   Siegel DJ, *The Developing Mind*, Guilford Publications, New York, 1999.

Chapter 5 Co-creation

1   'Environment', *Merriam Webster Dictionary*, Springfield, 2024.

Chapter 6 Friendship

1   Gottman JM and Gottman JS, 'The marriage survival kit: A research-based marital therapy', *Preventive Approaches in Couples Therapy*, Routledge, Philadelphia, 2012, pp. 304–330.

Chapter 7 Me to We

1   Hendrix H, 'Imago Couples Therapy with Harville Hendrix, Ph.D.: Proven Strategies for Helping Couples Connect, Heal and Grow', PESI, Eau Claire, 2012.

2   Real T, *Fierce Intimacy*, Sounds True Adult, Louisville, 2018.
3   Hendrix H and Hunt H, 'Imago relationship therapy: Creating a conscious marriage or relationship', *Preventive Approaches in Couples Therapy*, Routledge, Philadelphia, 2013, pp. 169–95.
4   Hendrix H et al., *Imago Relationship Therapy*, Wiley, New York, 2005.
5   Gottman JM et al., 'Four Horsemen in Couple and Family Therapy', *Encyclopedia of Couple and Family Therapy*, Springer, New York, 2019, pp. 1212–1216.
6   'Empathy', *Merriam Webster Dictionary*, Springfield, 2024.

Chapter 9 Clean Fighting

1   Gottman, JM and Gottman JS, *Gottman Method Couples Therapy Level 2: Assessment, Intervention, and Co-Morbidities*, (online professional training), the Gottman Institute, 2022.
2   Mellody P, *Facing Codependence: What It Is, Where It Comes from, How It Sabotages Our Lives*, HarperCollins, New York, 1989.
3   Gottman JM and Levenson RW, 'The timing of divorce: Predicting when a couple will divorce over a 14-year period', *Journal of Marriage and Family*, 62(3), 2000, pp. 737–45.
4   Gottman JM and Levenson RW, 'The timing of divorce: Predicting when a couple will divorce over a 14-year period', *Journal of Marriage and Family*, 62(3), 2000, pp. 737–45.
5   Gottman JM and Levenson RW, 'The timing of divorce: Predicting when a couple will divorce over a 14-year period', *Journal of Marriage and Family*, 62(3), 2000, pp. 737–45.
6   Gottman JM et al., 'Negative Sentiment Override in Couples and Families', *Encyclopedia of Couple and Family Therapy*, 2019, pp. 2019–2022.

Chapter 10 Bend and Mend

1   Gottman JM et al., 'Repair during marital conflict in newlyweds: How couples move from attack-defend to collaboration', *Journal of Family Psychotherapy*, 26(2), 2015, pp. 85–108.
2   Gottman JM et al., 'Repair during marital conflict in newlyweds: How couples move from attack-defend to collaboration', *Journal of Family Psychotherapy*, 26(2), 2015, pp. 85–108.
3   Gottman JM et al., 'Repair during marital conflict in newlyweds: How couples move from attack-defend to collaboration', *Journal of Family Psychotherapy*, 26(2), 2015, pp. 85–108.

Chapter 11 A Modern Sex Education

1   'Sexual attitudes', American Psychological Association, Washington, 2024.
2   Sævik KW and Konijnenberg C, 'The effects of sexual shame, emotion regulation and gender on sexual desire', *Scientific Reports*, 13(1), 2023, p. 4042.
3   Malkemus SA and Smith JF, 'Sexual Disembodiment: Sexual Energy, Trauma, and the Body', *Journal of Humanistic Psychology*, 2021.

4   Wenzel A, 'Basic strategies of cognitive behavioral therapy', *Psychiatric Clinics*, 40(4), 2017, pp. 597–609.
5   Metz ME and McCarthy BW, 'The "Good-Enough Sex" model for couple sexual satisfaction', *Sexual and Relationship Therapy*, 22(3), 2007, pp. 351–62.
6   Metz ME and McCarthy BW, 'The "Good-Enough Sex" model for couple sexual satisfaction', *Sexual and Relationship Therapy*, 22(3), 2007, pp. 351–62.

Chapter 12 Closeness and Intimacy

1   'Intimacy', *Merriam Webster Dictionary*, Springfield, 2024.
2   Dreisoerner A et al., 'Self-soothing touch and being hugged reduce cortisol responses to stress: A randomized controlled trial on stress, physical touch, and social identity', *Comprehensive Psychoneuroendocrinology*, 8, 2021, p. 100091.
3   Gottman J and Gottman J, 'The natural principles of love', *Journal of Family Theory & Review*, 9(1), 2017, pp. 7–26.
4   Gottman J and Gottman J, 'The natural principles of love', *Journal of Family Theory & Review*, 9(1), 2017, pp. 7–26.

Chapter 13 Demystifying Desire

1   Nagoski E, *Come As You Are*, Simon & Schuster, New York, 2015.
2   Nagoski E, *Come As You Are*, Simon & Schuster, New York, 2015.
3   Janssen E and Bancroft J, 'The dual control model: The role of sexual inhibition and excitation in sexual arousal and behavior', *The Psychophysiology of Sex*, 15, 2007, pp. 197–222.

Chapter 14 Embracing the Erotic

1   'Erotic', *Merriam Webster Dictionary*, Springfield, 2024.
2   'Erotic', *Merriam Webster Dictionary*, Springfield, 2024.

Index

Powered by Penguin

 Looking for more great reads, exclusive content and book giveaways? Subscribe to our weekly newsletter.

Scan the QR code or visit penguin.com.au/signup